OXFORD BIBL

General Ed
P. R. Ackroyd and C

THE OXFORD BIBLE SERIES

General Editors
Peter R. Ackroyd and Graham N. Stanton

The Old Testament: a Literary and Historical Introduction
Richard J. Coggins

Old Testament Narrative   David M. Gunn

Poets and Psalmists of the Old Testament   Peter R. Ackroyd

Prophecy and the Prophets of the Old Testament
John F. A. Sawyer

Wisdom and Law in the Old Testament   J. Blenkinsopp

The Origins of Christianity. A Historical Introduction to
the New Testament   Schuyler Brown

The Gospels and Jesus   Graham N. Stanton

Variety and Unity in New Testament Thought   J. Reumann

Pauline Christianity   John Ziesler

Biblical Interpretation   John Barton and Robert Morgan

The Origins of Christianity

A Historical Introduction to the New Testament

SCHUYLER BROWN

Oxford   New York

OXFORD UNIVERSITY PRESS

1984

Oxford University Press, Walton Street, Oxford OX2 6 DP

London Glasgow New York Toronto
Delhi Bombay Calcutta Madras Karachi
Kuala Lumpur Singapore Hong Kong Tokyo
Nairobi Dar es Salaam Cape Town
Melbourne Auckland

and associated companies in
Beirut Berlin Ibadan Mexico City Nicosia

Oxford is a trade mark of Oxford University Press

Published in the United States
by Oxford University Press, New York

British Library Cataloguing in Publication Data

Brown, Schuyler
The origins of Christianity: an historical
introduction to the New Testament. — (Oxford Bible
series)
1. Christianity
I. Title
200   BR121.2
ISBN 0-19-826202-7

Library of Congress Cataloging in Publication Data

Brown, Schuyler.
The origins of Christianity.
(Oxford Bible series)
Bibliography: p.
Includes indexes.
1. Bible. N.T. — Criticism, interpretation, etc.
2. Christianity—Origin.   I. Title.   II. Series.
BS2361.2.B76 1984   225.6'7   83-13436
ISBN 0-19-826202-7 (pbk.)

Typeset by Hope Services, Abingdon, Oxon
and printed in the United States of America

GENERAL EDITORS' PREFACE

There are many commentaries on individual books of the Bible, but the reader who wishes to take a broader view has less choice. This series is intended to meet this need. Its structure is thematic, with each volume embracing a number of biblical books. It is designed for use with any of the familiar translations of the Bible; quotations are normally from RSV, but the authors of the individual volumes also use other translations or make their own where this helps to bring out the particular meaning of a passage.

To provide general orientation, there are two volumes of a more introductory character: one will consider the Old Testament in its cultural and historical context, the other the New Testament, discussing the origins of Christianity. Four volumes deal with different kinds of material in the Old Testament: narrative, prophecy, poetry/psalmody, wisdom and law. Three volumes handle different aspects of the New Testament: the Gospels, Paul and Pauline Christianity, the varieties of New Testament thought. One volume looks at the nature of biblical interpretation, covering both Testaments.

The authors of the individual volumes write for a general readership. Technical terms and Hebrew or Greek words are explained; the latter are used only when essential to the understanding of the text. The general introductory volumes are designed to stand on their own, providing a framework, but also to serve to raise some of the questions which the remaining volumes examine in closer detail. All the volumes other than the two general ones include discussion of selected biblical passages in greater depth, thus providing examples of the ways in which the interpretation of the text makes possible deeper understanding of the wider issues, both historical and theological, with which the Bible is concerned. Select bibliographies in each volume point the way to further discussion of the many issues which remain open to fuller exploration.

P.R.A.
G.N.S.

NOTE

Unless otherwise indicated all biblical quotations in this publication have been taken from the Revised Standard Version of the Bible Copyrighted 1946, 1952, © 1971, 1973 by the Division of Christian Education of the National Council of the Churches of Christ in the United States of America, and are used by permission.

CONTENTS

1

Introduction

Spoken language is the principal means of communication between contemporaries. Written language makes possible our communication with the past. Among all the literary monuments from the past, some have achieved, at least within a particular culture, a normative status which makes them 'classics'. Of these classics, there are a few which have become *the* text in terms of which a culture seeks to understand itself and its continuing experience in history. For the ancient Greeks, Homer's *Iliad* and *Odyssey* held a unique position of pre-eminence. The devotion of the Jews to every letter of the Torah, that is, the Pentateuch or first five books of the Hebrew Bible, led to their being known as 'the people of the book'. The Bible, including the Old and New Testaments, has influenced Western civilization more than any other literary composition or collection. Within the English-speaking world, the influence of the Authorized Version is even greater than that of our greatest playwright, William Shakespeare.

Although the Bible comes to us from the past, it is read and interpreted in the present, and it is the Bible's continuing significance for each succeeding generation which has preserved its unique position, even in our secularist society. The Bible, like any literary work, has a life in history, and the shifting perceptions of its meaning, as it is passed on from age to age, are as much a part of it as the meaning intended by the original author or perceived by the original audience. The unchanging text generates an unending series of variant readings. Indeed, the history of Western civilization can be traced in the history of biblical interpretation.

Since the eighteenth century, the theological study of New Testament thought has gone hand in hand with an historical examination of Jesus and the movement which stemmed from him. For people today, all understanding, religious understanding included, is rooted in history, both the present historical situation *in which* we seek to understand and the past historical situation *of that which* we seek to understand.

Although, in the intention of their authors, the New Testament writings are documents of faith and religious instruction, they are also our principal source for whatever can be known about Jesus and the earliest church. References to Jesus and earliest Christianity which come from outside the Christian church are exceedingly rare and usually do no more than confirm what we already know from Christian sources. Since the New Testament has both theological and historical uses, it is important to be able to distinguish between them and to know the methodology which is appropriate to each use.

Historical interest is not the only, or even the primary, interest which motivates contemporary readers of the New Testament, and although the historical perspective has placed great weight on 'the intention of the author', it is actually the interest of the reader which determines how he approaches the text. This is not an endorsement of arbitrary subjectivism but a simple statement of fact. Only if we become aware of *our* expectations in approaching the text, can we formulate appropriate questions to address to the text and hope to hear answers from the text which are not simply echoes of what is already inside our own heads. A claim to objectivity or literalism which is unconscious of the interests which are actually motivating us, as we 'search the scriptures' (John 5: 39), leads to the worst possible subjectivism—the worst, because it is invincible.

The interests of twentieth-century men and women in the New Testament text are exceedingly varied. Besides the interest of the historian, there is the restricted, but entirely legitimate, interest of the philologist, who can learn a great deal from the New Testament about the state of the Greek language in the first century of the Common Era. (See below for the explanation of this expression.) The fact that the New Testament can provide answers to the questions of a philologist, even though philological interests seem to have been quite foreign to the New Testament authors themselves, illustrates a point which is absolutely crucial for our investigation: the interest or lack of interest of a New Testament writer in the questions with which we are concerned has no direct bearing on whether or not we may be able to find answers to these questions through the study of a New Testament book.

Of course, there will be many things about Jesus and the early church about which the New Testament writings can provide no help to the historian. However, Bultmann's assertion that 'we can know practically nothing about Jesus' life and personality, *because* [emphasis ours] the Christian sources had no interest in such matters' is a *non sequitur*, even if we could accept without qualification the reason he gives for his initial statement. The fact that Rembrandt painted in an era before the discovery of ultra-violet light does not prohibit the modern art historian from using this or any other scientific technique which may answer questions about the artist's life and work.

Of course, the unique position of the Bible in Western culture is not simply that of a classic. The Bible is a *religious* classic, and this explains why it is of special interest to the theologian, the believer, and the searcher. It is this interest which, for all the differences of culture and outlook, unites those who read the Bible today with readers of previous generations, who did not share the more specialized concerns of twentieth-century historians or philologists. Nevertheless, we may not omit a historical treatment of Jesus and the early Church and pass immediately to a consideration of the religious affirmations which the New Testament books contain. Such a short circuit would not do justice to New Testament interpretation in our time and place. The attempt to understand Jesus and the Christian movement as past historical phenomena is both legitimate and necessary, even though it involves adopting, towards the subject of our investigation, a neutral attitude which was foreign to the New Testament writers and the world in which they lived.

In the Biblical references which follow, parallel gospel passages are given simply as 'par.'. By using a synopsis, such as B. H. Throckmorton's *Gospel Parallels*, the student can readily find the parallel(s) to the passage cited.

The terms 'AD', i.e. *anno Domini* ('in the year of the Lord'), and 'BC', i.e. 'before Christ', which assume a Christian standpoint, are replaced with 'CE', i.e. 'Common Era', and 'BCE', i.e. 'before the Common Era' which are neutral, and make no such assumption. The system of dating according to 'the Christian era' goes back to Dionysius Exiguus, a Scythian monk who lived in Rome *c.* 500–50. According to both Matthew (2: 1) and Luke (1: 5), Herod the Great was still alive at the time of Jesus' birth. Since the king died in 4 BCE, the year 1 CE is clearly not the actual date of Jesus' birth. The discrepancy is the result of Dionysius' miscalculation.

2

History and the New Testament

Christianity and the rise of historical consciousness

In a second introduction to his work, after the cycle of stories about the birth of Jesus and the Baptist, the third evangelist lists the leaders, both secular and sacred, during whose period in office 'the word of God came to John' (Luke 3: 2). At the head of the list is the name of the Roman emperor, Tiberius Caesar, followed by the 'governor', i.e. the prefect, of Judaea, Pontius Pilate (v. 1). The mention of the emperor, to whose authority Paul will appeal in the second volume of Luke's work (Acts 25: 11), reflects the author's conviction that the narrative which he is about to relate of 'the things which have been accomplished among us' (Luke 1: 1) has worldwide significance. The story of Jesus and of the early church has not taken place 'in a corner' (Acts 26: 26). Christianity is being presented as an historical phenomenon.

For those whose entire history and culture have been affected by the emergence of a Jewish sect (cf. Acts 24: 5, 14; 28: 22) upon the stage of world history, the historical significance of Christianity is so obvious that it may seem odd that this significance is recognized for the first time in a book which does not seem to have been written until the last decade of the first century. We therefore need to recall that for the earliest Christians the 'new covenant' (Luke 22: 20; 1 Cor. 11: 25; 2 Cor. 3: 6) to which they belonged marked the end of history (cf. 1 Cor. 7: 29, 31) rather than the beginning of a new historical epoch.

In a cartoonist's drawing, a group of American Indians is represented rushing to greet Columbus and his crew as they arrive at the island of Hispaniola in the New World. The caption reads: 'Thank God! We've been discovered.' The point, of course, is that we cannot assume that the modern historian's perspective, in this case, the importance of the discovery of America, was shared by the persons who are the subject of his enquiry.

The first followers of Jesus were quite unconscious that they were making history. When the modern historian investigates the origins of Christianity, he not only goes beyond the viewpoint and methods of ancient historians, but his enterprise is marked by a historical consciousness which was largely absent from the self-understanding of those whom he is studying. The history which culminated in the 'last days' (Acts 2: 17) inaugurated by Jesus' death and resurrection was not the secular sort written by the Greek authors whose style Luke imitates in his prologue (Luke 1: 1-4). The earliest Christians saw their movement as the climax of the history of salvation—'the mighty works of God' (Acts 2: 11)—narrated in 'the scriptures', i.e. the books of the Old Testament.

Jesus of Nazareth, like John the Baptist before him, left behind no writings to record his activities or to preserve his teachings. The earliest Christian author whose works have survived, the apostle Paul, did not write with posterity in mind. Most of his epistles are a substitute for his physical presence when he is separated from the communities which he has founded (cf. 2 Cor. 10: 10). The principal issues which he addresses are those which have arisen within the life of these same communities (cf. 1 Cor. 7: 1; 8: 1, 12: 1; 15: 12).

Only towards the end of the century, when the first generation of disciples had passed away (cf. Mark 13: 30 par.) and the Lord had still not returned, did Christians come to view themselves as part of a wider history and look ahead to the fate of their community in a hostile world. The use of the word 'Christian' expresses a new consciousness of the historical significance of the movement as something distinct from both Judaism and the other cults of the Graeco-Roman world. It is surely no accident that of the three occurrences of this word in the New Testament, two are to be found in the book of Acts (11: 26; 26: 28).

Past and future in the New Testament

For the first Christians, Jesus of Nazareth was no dead figure from the past. They experienced his presence in the gatherings of the community (Matt. 18: 20; cf. 28: 20), and they anticipated his imminent return (1 Cor. 11: 26; 16: 22; Rev. 22: 20). Nevertheless, it is an exaggeration when scholars suggest that the first Christians had little or no interest in the past. In our earliest extant profession of faith all the verbs are in the past tense: 'Christ died . . . was buried . . . was raised . . . and appeared' (1 Cor. 15: 3-4). Moreover, since the first 'article' of this creed, that the Messiah had died, was 'a stumbling block to Jews and folly to Gentiles' (1 Cor. 1: 23), it could not be credibly proclaimed without some explanation of how Christ, the redeemer king, had happened to end his life on a cross. The church's *kerygma* (the Greek word for 'proclamation') necessitated reflection on the past.

The earliest extended narrative in the gospels, the passion story, seems to owe its existence to this need to explain past events. To be sure, this explanation is historical only in a restricted sense. The narrative's main concern is theological: the scriptural references, whether full citations or brief allusions, are intended to convince the reader that Christ's death was willed by God. Nevertheless, the story also illustrates, on the human level, how the Jewish leaders managed to persuade the people to demand and obtain Jesus' crucifixion.

Earlier in the first three gospels, a collection of controversies between Jesus and the Jewish leaders depicts the growing hostility which culminates in a decision to put Jesus to death (Mark 3: 6 par.). Here too historical motivation is discernible. The composition of Mark's gospel, generally agreed to be the oldest, seems occasioned in part by the desire to preserve the variety of traditional materials which the gospel incorporates, materials which were perceived to be in danger of being lost. Our suggestion that Luke-Acts is the earliest Christian writing to reflect a developed historical consciousness must therefore be coupled with an acknowledgement that Christianity was a historical religion from the start, in so far as its basic proclamation was concerned with past events and led to reflection upon these events.

The rise of modern historiography

The task of the modern historian is often described as aiming at an objective reconstruction of the past. Although the word 'history'

(Greek *historia* = 'enquiry') has been used from ancient times until the present, modern historiography has its origins in the nineteenth century. This century was a great age for facts, and one of its leading scholars, Leopold von Ranke, defined the historian's task as 'simply to show how it really was'. The nineteenth century was preoccupied with names, places, dates, occurrences, sequences, causes, effects. It found its ideal of historical objectivity in the natural scientist's investigation of physical phenomena.

Although there is no desire today to return to the sort of moralizing history against which von Ranke was protesting, we are now aware that the historian stands within the history which he is investigating, so that total objectivity is unattainable. The historian must get his facts straight, but this is not his sole or ultimate objective. He must also know how to select the right facts, namely those which shed light on the particular historical phenomenon which he is investigating. It is in the selection, ordering, and evaluation of historical data that the historian's task principally consists, and so the reconstruction of the past must ultimately depend upon his judgement.

In selecting his material, the historian is guided by his personal criteria of significance. There can be no such thing as historiography without presuppositions; all research involves a 'pre-understanding' which influences the scholar in the questions he asks and the judgements he makes. Nevertheless, propagandist history is perceived to be a betrayal of the craft, and the suppression, distortion, or fabrication of evidence is the unforgivable sin. Historical writing which serves to justify the personal ideology of the author is always suspect, and the greater the historian's ability to rise above the limited vision of his own situation, the greater the significance and impact of his work.

The sources for earliest Christianity

The writings of the New Testament are the principal source for the investigation of the Christian movement during the first century of its existence. Archaeology has investigated the sites mentioned in the New Testament and given us valuable insights into the historical context of Jesus' ministry and the world in which Christianity arose. Nevertheless, archaeological finds shed little direct light on the history of the Christian movement itself during its first century (*c*.30–130). Apart from their religious beliefs, there was nothing to distinguish the first Christians from the Jews, Greeks, or Romans among whom they lived. They did not construct special places of prayer but assembled in private homes (Acts 12: 12; Col. 4: 15). Their simple worship required no distinctive ritual objects, and the scriptures they used were those of the synagogue. A Christian house-chapel with a painted baptistry has been discovered at Dura Europos, far to the northeast of Palestine, in the great bend of the Euphrates River, but it dates from the third century.

A spectacular archaeological discovery has illustrated the use of the cross as a religious symbol in the first Christian century. In the town of Herculaneum, which was destroyed in 79 by an eruption of Vesuvius, a chamber was uncovered in the 1930s which revealed on one wall a square covered with plaster. In it was deeply engraved the sign of a Latin cross, which had been violently torn out of its place just before the destruction of the site. This exceptional discovery proves the rule that the historian of Christian origins is dependent upon the evidence of literary monuments, particularly the writings of the New Testament. Archaeological finds have been cited as evidence for the reliability of certain details in New Testament narratives, for example the healing of the paralytic at the pool of Bethzatha (John 5: 1–8) or Paul's first missionary journey, according to Acts 13: 4 – 14: 28. However, if such evidence is accepted, it is not a source of new historical knowledge of Christian origins, since it merely confirms what the New Testament sources tell us.

There is no rule of history that human institutions must undergo critical points of evolution at the beginning of a new century, and so the question arises why the 'origins' of Christianity are to be confined to the years between Jesus' crucifixion (*c*.30) and the probable date of composition of the last New Testament book (*c*.130). Is there not a certain circularity at work here? We restrict the period under investigation to a time for which we are mainly dependent on the evidence of the New Testament and then complain of the difficulties which this dependence creates.

The 'apostolic age' and the 'apostolic writings'

In the third book of his *Ecclesiastical History* Eusebius (*c.* 260-340) writes: 'We have now described the facts which have come to our knowledge concerning the apostles and their times, and the sacred writings which they have left us' (xxxi. 6). The historical significance of the years 30–130 comes from the special importance which later writers give to the Christian literature which dates from this period. The Eusebian triad—the apostles, apostolic times, apostolic writings —is illuminating. The historian has difficulty assessing the personal influence of 'the apostles', who, apart from Peter and Paul, have no clear role in the post-Easter community. But he has no problem in tracing the stages by which the 'apostolic writings', that is, the New Testament books, were accorded normative authority by the church of the second, third, and fourth centuries.

All twenty-seven books of the New Testament were connected by the early church with 'the apostles'. Modern critical scholarship has cast doubt on the traditional authorship of all the New Testament writings, with the exception of seven Pauline letters (Rom., 1-2 Cor., Gal., Phil., 1 Thess., Philem.). All the other books may be either anonymous or pseudonymous. But for the church of the second and succeeding centuries these twenty-seven books emanated directly or indirectly from 'the apostles', and, as 'apostolic writings', the teaching which they contain was considered normative for all succeeding ages. Hence, in the self-understanding of the Christian church, the period from 30 to 130, in which these books were written, was not simply the first period in the church's history; it was the foundational period upon which the church's entire history depended.

The special character of 'the apostolic writings' and the period during which they were composed is reflected in the fact that the literary forms used in the New Testament were not continued in the later period. Once the formation of the New Testament canon had been completed, the composition of epistles, gospels, apocalypses, and acts was terminated within orthodox circles; non-canonical writings which were cast in these forms became automatically suspect. The early patristic literature is dominated by apologetic concerns and makes use of other literary forms, borrowed from non-Christian authors.

The problem of 'origins' in modern historiography

There is, then, a certain legitimacy in taking the period of Christian 'origins' to be those decades during which its normative literature was composed. Nevertheless, the concern for 'origins', which has had a special place in historical thinking, has certain dangers attached to it. All too often the 'origins' are assumed to be the cause of everything that follows. But whatever the special significance given by the Christian church to its canonical literature, the historian cannot regard it or the period of its composition as providing an explanation for the subsequent history of Christianity. For although constant reference is made to the New Testament books throughout the history of the Christian church, what the history of biblical interpretation principally reveals is the development of Christianity, and the historical causes for this development can certainly not be reduced to the influence of the canonical Christian scripture.

Every society, civil or sacred, tells stories about the way in which it came to be the way it is. By rooting present practices in the will of a divine founder, the impression is given that they are in accordance with the nature of things and essential to the well-being of the community. An appeal to past 'origins' to justify present faith and practice has been characteristic of the church's use of scripture until very recently. Christians have sought to legitimate new developments by finding them in their normative literature and, indeed, by tracing them back to the will of Jesus himself.

The critical function of historiography

The reconstruction of the origins of Christianity which the historian proposes inevitably calls into question such self-legitimating accounts, as well as the use of the New Testament evidence on which they are based. Even if the historian is a Christian, his investigation is not concerned with legitimating subsequent historical developments or any particular Christian body. Indeed, the past which he reconstructs may well have the effect of calling contemporary Christian self-understanding into question, with the result that new developments become possible.

The canonical status of the New Testament writings does not assure the historian that they contain the kind of truth for which he is looking. For him the significance of canonicity lies rather in having preserved certain documents of early Christianity and not others. The fact that the church of the second and later centuries found a satisfactory expression of its faith in the writings preserved in the canon forced many other literary monuments out of circulation and into oblivion, monuments which, if preserved, would have made possible a far more adequate reconstruction of the earliest stages of the Christian movement. The New Testament writings reveal, to the critical eye, a greater pluralism than was tolerated by the orthodoxy which canonized them. Nevertheless, the fact that the formation of the canon was part of a tendency towards such orthodoxy cautions us against assuming that it represents the full spectrum of belief and practice during the first century of the Christian movement. Significant voices were almost certainly excluded from the canonical selection. The recent discovery of the Nag Hammadi library with its large number of Gnostic writings has given us a new realization of how varied the forms of early Christianity actually were (see also pp. 151-2).

The social history of earliest Christianity: reading between the lines

Not only do the New Testament writings offer a limited sampling, determined by later orthodoxy, of the religious thinking of the first Christians; their very character as religious literature is a problem for the historian. For such literature is only one aspect of the movement which produced it. No one would seek to understand the Protestant Reformation simply by reading the works of Luther, Calvin, and other theologians, while ignoring documents which cast light on the social history of the movement. But the lack of such documentation for first-century Christianity forces the historian back to the New Testament even to answer questions of a non-religious character.

To be able to do so at all, the historian must learn to 'eavesdrop' on the New Testament authors; he must read between the lines. If he is to uncover traces of the life—and not only the beliefs—of the first Christian communities, he must listen for things which the authors reveal only in passing or even unintentionally. In this he operates in the same way as historians of all periods. For historical research has come to place special confidence in evidence which the documents give in spite of themselves. Conscious and deliberate testimony is always open to the suspicion of intending to convey the views of the witness, rather than an account of what actually took place. Unintentional evidence may be erroneous, but at least one can exclude any desire to deceive.

Historical criticism and the testimony of religious writers

Of course, such a way of speaking is anachronistic when applied to the New Testament authors, in so far as historical objectivity is a modern ideal. The moral overtones inherent in the word 'deception' are out of place when dealing, for example, with the phenomenon of pseudonymity in the New Testament. The author of the Pastoral Epistles did not think he was acting dishonestly when he circulated 1 and 2 Timothy and Titus under the name of Paul. Convinced, as he was, that his teaching was also the teaching of the apostle, he used Paul's name and authority to confirm in the truth those to whom and for whose benefit he was writing.

Nevertheless, to assume that an author's religious sincerity is a sufficient guarantee for what he says would totally undermine the modern historian's task. Historical truth may not be the only, or even the most important, kind of truth, but it is the truth for which the historian is responsible. In the case in question, he cannot be led by 'Paul's' seemingly untendentious personal remarks (2 Tim. 4: 9-21; Titus 3: 12-13) to postulate the apostle's return to the East after his Roman house arrest (Acts 28: 16, 30-1). Material which may have served to reinforce the fiction of Pauline authorship cannot be used to reconstruct the apostle's ministry.

Ancient historiography

Such problems are common to all areas of ancient history, and it would be naïve to expect them to be absent from the study of

Christian origins. Ancient historical writers did not view their task in the same way as their modern counterparts; their criteria of significance were quite different. The ancient historian was more concerned with transmitting to his readers what seemed important, useful, or edifying than in reconstructing the past. Instruction by example, whether good or bad, was a major motive in writing 'history'. The ancient historiographer did not share our scruples about passing moral judgements on past personalities and events, nor did he feel obliged to document everything in his account. He freely composed speeches expressing his own perception of the significance of past events and placed them on the lips of the main actors in the historical drama. Ancient historiography was aristocratic both in its selection of subject matter and in its norms of evaluation. Attention was focused on prominent persons and the political changes which they brought about, not on what we today call social history. Moreover, since moral judgements were often based on what was good or bad for the social class from which the writer himself came, many classical works of ancient historiography would, according to contemporary standards, be classified as crude propaganda.

The problem of source material

The historian of Christian origins also shares with other students of ancient history the problem of reconstructing a past for which the sources are either fragmentary or missing altogether. Although the loss or destruction of documents is possible at any time, generally speaking the more remote the period under investigation, the more serious the damage done to the historian's sources. The spectacular discoveries of long-buried archives remain the exception rather than the rule.

Besides the ravages of time and the effect of canonicity, the high cost of writing materials in antiquity has contributed to the impoverishment of our knowledge of the past, by promoting a tendency, observable in the New Testament itself, to abbreviate earlier documents, rather than to reproduce them in full. Since the available sources are so meagre, the historian must try to read as much out of them as possible. Often he is forced to conjecture, filling in the gaps in his material in much the same way as a palaeographer fills in the lacunae in a damaged manuscript.

This problem of sources is so basic that it may not be going too far to suggest that the study of ancient history (Christian origins included) is qualitatively different from the study of more recent periods. For though all contemporary historians may share a common professional ideal, the vast differences in the availability of source material result in this ideal being variously realized, according to the period under investigation. To obtain answers to certain kinds of historical questions, the availability of eye-witnesses is a virtual necessity. A contemporary British biographer recently observed that he preferred subjects who had relatives and friends still living. On the other hand, certain other kinds of historical questions cannot be answered until there is sufficient distance from the events under investigation for their consequences to have become apparent. An essential task of the historian is to formulate the questions appropriate to the material at his disposal and to determine with what degree of probability he is able to answer them.

The problem of canonicity

Besides the problems which he shares with all other students of ancient history, the historian of Christian origins encounters particular difficulties which result from the canonical status of his source material. Whether or not the historian himself is a believing Christian, his account of Christian origins will be read by those whose approach to the New Testament writings is influenced by their Christian faith. Before the development of modern historical methods towards the end of the eighteenth century, it was assumed that the literal sense of biblical narrative always referred to historical occurrences. At this point a critical distinction was introduced between the biblical narrative and the 'reality' which it depicts. The pre-critical unity of history and biblical narrative was shattered.

Fundamentalism and exaggerated scepticism

Many believing Christians have yet to make their peace with this development. They fail to see how a critical approach is compatible with the reverence which the biblical text demands. One can appreciate this difficulty. Christianity is a 'historical' religion, that is, a faith whose fundamental credal affirmations are expressed in the past tense. Since we are dependent upon the New Testament writings for our access to those past events which are the object of Christian faith, a distinction between what these writings tell us and what 'really' happened seems to pose a threat to faith. This problem is compounded by the ecclesiastical dogmas of verbal inspiration and inerrancy, which appear to rule out *a priori* a critical approach to the New Testament.

At the opposite end of the spectrum from the approach of many traditional Christians is the position of Rudolf Bultmann, who considers the sole object of faith to be the Christ event—Jesus' death on the cross. Jesus himself belongs to the history of Judaism; his preaching is simply the presupposition for the proclamation of the church. This proclamation has no content; it does not communicate information; rather, it is a summons to authentic existence, which Bultmann understands in terms of existentialist philosophy. In his view, history is irrelevant for faith just as the works of the law are irrelevant for salvation, which comes through faith alone. Such faith can have no support outside itself.

Bultmann's hermeneutics leads naturally to extreme historical scepticism. If the reconstruction of the past is irrelevant for faith, if the New Testament is a form of the *kerygma*, rather than a source for what happened, then the less history it contains, the better. In his book on Jesus Bultmann affirms: 'I am of the opinion that we can know practically nothing about Jesus' life and personality, since the Christian sources had no interest in such matters, besides being very fragmentary and overgrown with legend, and since no other sources exist.' Bultmann's pre-eminence and influence have led many contemporary New Testament scholars to join in his flight from history. The theologian's search for a certitude which faith alone can provide continually obstructs an impartial evaluation of the evidence.

If the historian of Christian origins is to be faithful to his task, he must steer a course between the uncritical acceptance of the biblical narrative demanded by fundamentalism and a theologically motivated scepticism, whose hypercritical approach ignores the rules of historical probability and is as uncritical, in its own way, as the opposite extreme. A critical reading of the sources is the only one possible for the historian, if he is to use the New Testament writings to reconstruct the past. He has no choice but to ask whether things really happened in the way in which they are represented in his material. But before the historian can evaluate the evidence, he must first identify the historical material contained in his sources. For the New Testament, as a collection of religious writings, contains many affirmations about which the historian is not competent to make a judgement: affirmations concerning God's existence, God's intervention in the world's affairs, or, speaking anthropomorphically, the effect on God produced by actions which occur in this world.

There are some historians who go so far as to maintain that historical method and religious belief are incompatible. They argue that the historian's task can only be carried out in a world in which the phenomena are not interfered with by divine interventions. For unless the operation of inscrutable and incalculable divine causes can be excluded, no calculation of probable causes is possible. However, divine and historical causality do not operate on the same level. Consequently, there is no need for the historian to deny the existence of God or God's activity in the world. However, he may not include such divine activity in his explanation of historical events. His proper task is a 'horizontal' explanation which neither denies nor takes into consideration the possible operation of 'vertical' influences.

Historical affirmations and faith affirmations

Obviously, religious beliefs are included within the historian's competence in so far as he must determine their meaning and make a judgement concerning when and by whom they were entertained. However, he should refrain from expressing any opinion on their truth or falsehood. If we return to the early creed cited by Paul, we see that it contains historical affirmations, faith affirmations, and one affirmation which seems to occupy an intermediate position. Without going into a detailed exegesis, we may say that 1 Cor. 15: 3-5 affirms, explicitly or implicitly, that

1. Jesus is the Christ.
2. He died.
3. He died for our sins, i.e. his death brought about their forgiveness.
4. He was buried.
5. He was raised from the dead by God.
6. He appeared to Peter and other witnesses.

We shall leave out of our consideration 'according to the scriptures', which occurs twice, and 'on the third day', since the precise meaning of these phrases is disputed.

1. Although etymologically 'Christ' means 'anointed', the first affirmation obviously does not refer to an observable rite, such as the anointing of an Israelite king (1 Sam. 10: 1) or high priest (Lev. 8: 12). In the last centuries before the Common Era the term had come to mean '*the* anointed', that is, the redeemer king who was expected to restore the kingdom of Israel. In Christian usage, the term underwent a significant change, which is brought out in affirmation number 3. However, even its Jewish use implies a faith statement, in so far as the person to whom the title is applied is believed to be acting as God's agent and for God's purposes.

2. The statement that Jesus died is a historical affirmation. Of course, any human being who lived two thousand years ago may be presumed to have died. Therefore, the historian need not depend upon the witnesses to Jesus' death mentioned in Mark 15: 40-1 par. The historical significance of the statement lies in its presupposition, namely, that Jesus existed, that he was a historical person. Apart from a few Soviet ideologists and some humanists, whose interest is more anti-religious than historical, hardly any serious scholar today denies that Jesus did exist.

3. The statement that Jesus' death brought about a change in the relationship between humankind and God, consisting in God's forgiveness of our sins, is clearly a faith statement not susceptible to objective verification (cf. Mark 2: 9-12 par.).

4. This statement, which needs to be carefully distinguished from the affirmation of the *empty* tomb (Luke 24: 2-3, 12, 23), is clearly a statement of historical fact. The historian must determine its truth by examining the brief account of Jesus' burial (Mark 15: 42-6), to

which the names of two witnesses have been added (v. 47). It is worth observing that even Bultmann found no reason to question the basic historicity of this account. The only verses which raise any doubts are vv. 44-5, which could have been inserted to counter objections that Jesus was buried after only apparent death and are missing in the Matthean and Lucan versions of the burial. Though Acts 13: 29 differs from Mark in the persons designated as having carried out Jesus' burial (cf. v. 27), it confirms the fact of the burial itself.

5. Since the passive construction, 'Christ has been raised', implies God as the agent, this is clearly a faith statement. There is no passage in the New Testament which names any witness to the actual resurrection of Jesus. The earliest text to do so is the *Gospel of Peter* (8: 39-40) (M. R. James, *The Apocryphal New Testament*, p. 92), where the witnesses to Jesus leaving the tomb are the soldiers (contrast Matt. 28: 4).

6. This concluding affirmation of the pre-Pauline creed is difficult to categorize. Jesus' appearance after his death is better attested than many events in ancient history which we accept without question. Paul is able to refer the Corinthians to a large number of witnesses, most of whom were still alive at the time that he wrote to the community (v. 6) and could be consulted. It is the extraordinary nature of this appearance, not any defect in its attestation, which has caused scepticism. The testimony itself can be verified by the historian, but its content is an immediate personal experience, not subject, even at the time, to confirmation by anyone outside the circle of those 'chosen by God as witnesses' (Acts 10: 41). The fact that all these witnesses were Christians, who came to believe in Jesus' messiahship precisely through his appearance to them, makes the content of this affirmation a faith experience, about which the historian can only speculate. Was it a personal encounter with someone who had died? Was it a hallucination, prompted by the shame of having denied the Master? Was it a faith insight into Jesus' true significance during his lifetime? A judgement in this matter is likely to depend more on the historian's philosophical and religious convictions than on his competence as a historian. Nevertheless, the problem of the historian's attitude to extraordinary events

attested in his sources is an important one to which we shall have to return.

From our analysis it is clear that although faith affirmations and historical affirmations can often be distinguished, they are not unrelated to each other. The affirmation that Christ died for our sins presupposes the affirmation that Jesus died, which, in turn, presupposes that he lived. Since there were no witnesses to Jesus' resurrection from the dead, the affirmation that it occurred depends on the affirmation of Jesus' appearance after his death. Thus, while faith statements are not capable of historical verification, which would make them cease to be faith statements (cf. Heb. 11: 1), they are capable, theoretically, of historical falsification. The relationship between faith and history is more complex than Bultmann's hermeneutics suggests.

The presuppositions for the two faith statements in this creed, namely Jesus' death and the apostolic testimony to his appearance after death, cannot be disproved on historical grounds. But is Jesus' death the *only* presupposition for the faith statement that Christ died for our sins? If the interpretation were correct that Jesus actually was a political insurgent and was justly executed as such, or that the end of his life broke in upon him as a completely unforeseen catastrophe, that would, in fact, have been fatal for the faith of the first Christians in the Christ whom they proclaimed.

Does Christian faith today require that Jesus died with trust in God and an inner acceptance of his death as divinely willed? As we saw earlier, the passion narrative is concerned to show that Jesus' suffering and death were in accordance with God's will. There is no interest in depicting Jesus' state of mind. Mark's citation of Ps. 22: 1, 'My God, my God, why hast thou forsaken me?' (Mark 15: 34 par.), suggests that Jesus' plight on the cross fulfils the scriptures and is part of God's saving plan (cf. Mark 10: 45 par.). Consequently, the cry of abandonment cannot be used in support of Bultmann's suggestion that Jesus died in despair. But it is equally questionable to suggest that the psalm, which includes a prayer for divine help (vv. 19-21) and the psalmist's thanksgiving after help has been received (v. 22), establishes that Jesus died at peace with God (cf. Luke 23: 46). From a historical point of view, we can say nothing with certainty about Jesus' interior state on the cross. Of course, we have sayings from Jesus' ministry which express his attitude towards God, and one may conjecture that this attitude remained unchanged despite what befell him during the last days of his life. However, such conjectures do not have the certitude required by the faith affirmation itself.

The tension between history and faith would be even greater if Jesus' saving death were taken to presuppose his clear foreknowledge of the resurrection (cf. Mark 8: 31 par.). For it is difficult to recon-cile the historicity of such an explicit prediction either with the disciples' incomprehension at the time (Mark 9: 9-10) or with their reaction to Jesus' arrest (Mark 14: 50 par.) and the news of his resurrection (Luke 24: 11).

Faith affirmations and historical affirmations often differ in their content, but this is not always the case. For example, the view that Jesus should die as Messiah belongs to the dogmatic motifs of the passion story. But because the motif is dogmatic, it does not follow that it is necessarily unhistorical. Indeed, Nils Dahl argues that the only plausible explanation for the proclamation after Easter of Jesus *as the Christ* is to be found in the inscription on the cross: he was executed on the charge of having been 'the king of the Jews' (Mark 15: 26), a political insurgent. The Easter experience disproved the false charge against Jesus, but it did more than that: it gave a new meaning to the charge on the cross. Jesus *was* indeed the king of the Jews, but in an altogether different sense: he was the Messiah king who would save his people from their sins (cf. Matt. 1: 21). In this case, the historical fact is the presupposition for the faith affirmation.

Faith affirmations and historical affirmations also differ in their degree of certitude. Given the nature of his evidence, there is little that the historian of Christian origins can affirm with anything more than some degree of probability. The numinous certainty of faith must come from another source.

Dating the New Testament books

Having discussed the problems which arise from Christian origins being 1) a part of ancient history and 2) an object of contemporary theological interest, we shall now consider the nature of the evidence which is at the historian's disposal. Just as there are few archaeological or inscriptional finds which cast light on the earliest years of the Christian movement, so too no autographs of Christian writings from this period have been preserved. The earliest fragment we possess is P^{52}, which contains a few verses from the Fourth Gospel and has been dated to the first half of the second century.

Since the historian cannot ascertain the age of the New Testament books from the age of the manuscripts, he is forced to rely on indications in the texts themselves. In antiquity, official letters often included the date of writing, but we do not find this information in any of the New Testament books. We must therefore depend on the sort of indirect evidence which we mentioned earlier. The New Testament authors had little occasion to point out to their readers that they were writing at such and such a time, and references to recent or contemporary events of world history are exceedingly rare. One datable event which had profound implications for the Christian movement was the destruction of Jerusalem by the Romans in the year 70 CE. The burning of the temple, the centre of Jewish worship, is narrated by Josephus in *The Jewish War* (*BJ* VI. 4. 5-7), and this catastrophe came to be perceived by Christians as God's judgement on Pharisaic Judaism (cf. Matt. 23: 32-9). Many questions of dating involve the presence or absence in the New Testament books of allusions to this crucial event.

New Testament references to the fall of Jerusalem

In the Lucan eschatological discourse Jesus warns the disciples: 'But when you see Jerusalem surrounded by armies, then know that its desolation has come near' (Luke 21: 20). This explicit reference to the siege of the holy city (cf. Josephus, *BJ* V) would seem to be a prophecy after the event, particularly since it replaces the cryptic allusion in the Marcan parallel to the presence of someone 'where he ought not to be', i.e. in the temple (Mark 13: 14; cf. Dan. 9: 27; 12: 11; 2 Thess. 2: 3-10).

Jesus' prophecy of the temple's destruction in Mark (13: 2) has also been taken by some scholars as a prophecy after the event, but here the case is less clear. If this passage was composed after the temple had been destroyed by fire, it is hard to see why a prophecy of the *razing* of the building (cf. 2 Sam. 17: 13) should have been placed on Jesus' lips. Moreover, since there are predictions of the temple's destruction in the Old Testament (e.g. Jer. 26: 6, 18 (= Mic. 3: 12); 1 Kgs. 9: 8), as well as in rabbinic literature (Jer. Joma 43ᶜ; cf. Josephus, *BJ* VI. 5. 3), there is nothing incredible in such a saying coming from Jesus. Indeed, one of the charges at his trial concerns just such a prophecy (Mark 14: 58 par.).

The same words occur in Matthew (24: 2), immediately after the evangelist's 'woes against the Pharisees' (23: 1-36) and the 'lament over Jerusalem' (23: 37-9). But the evidence that Matthew is looking back on the holy city's destruction is stronger than in the case of Mark, since Matthew has inserted into the parable of the marriage feast (Matt. 22: 1-14) what appears to be an allegorical reference to this event. In response to the action of the invited guests, who had killed his servants, 'the king was angry, and he sent his troops and destroyed those murderers and burned their city' (22: 7).

The references to the destruction of Jerusalem in Matthew and Luke seem clear enough for these works to be dated with confidence after 70. In the case of Mark, however, opinions differ as to whether his gospel was written just before or just after that fateful year. Mark 13: 7 ('When you hear of wars and rumours of war, do not be alarmed') seems to refer to the Jewish War, but it is not entirely clear whether the climactic event in this war has already taken place.

Finally, the words in 1 Thess. 2: 16, 'But at last God's wrath has come upon them', i.e. the Jews (v. 14), have been taken as a reference to Jerusalem's destruction. It seems scarcely necessary to see such a specific allusion here, but if the passage is taken in this way, then 1 Thessalonians, or, at least, the section in which these words occur (2: 13-16) cannot have been written by Paul, whose martyrdom seems to have preceded the Jewish War.

Conservative scholars have seen in the absence of any clear reference in the Fourth Gospel to the destruction of Jerusalem an indication of its early composition. The Johannine parallel to Mark 13: 2, 'Destroy this temple, and in three days I will raise it up'

(John 2: 19), is explained by the evangelist in terms of the temple of Jesus' body (v. 21). However, there are other indications that John is the latest of the gospels. In post-70 Judaism, under the leadership of the Pharisees, the confession of Jesus as the Messiah became grounds for exclusion from the synagogue, and this development, which contrasts with Pharisaic toleration of observant Jewish Christians before the war (cf. Acts 5: 34-9), seems to be reflected in the agreement referred to in John 9: 22 (cf. 12: 42; 16: 2).

The extensive critique of the levitical priesthood in the Letter to the Hebrews would take on special significance if this work had been written in the situation following the destruction of Jerusalem and the end of sacrificial functioning by priests. However, the text gives no clear answer to the question whether the holy city is still standing and the temple cult still going on. The author's argument refers not to the worship of the Herodian temple but to the cultic prescriptions for the tent of meeting used during Israel's wilderness wanderings.

Literary and theological evidence

So, despite the significance of the year 70 for Christianity's separation from Judaism, we cannot expect every New Testament book composed after that date to contain a clear reference to Jerusalem's destruction. Fortunately, the historian has other things to go on, such as indications of literary dependence of one New Testament book on another and signs of theological development. Of course, such evidence only enables the historian to date one New Testament book in relation to another. Thus, if Matthew and Luke have used Mark as a source, as is generally believed, it follows that they must have been written after Mark, but an absolute dating will depend upon the dating of the Marcan source, which, as we have seen, is only approximate.

One reason for considering John to be the latest of the gospels is his 'high' christology. The Johannine Christ's use of the divine name, 'I am' at, for example John 8: 24, 58 (see below, p. 115), and his affirmation of oneness with the Father (10: 30) have no precise parallels in the first three, or 'synoptic', gospels (but cf. Matt. 11: 27 par.). During the first decades of the Christian movement there was no single norm for 'orthodoxy', and various expressions of belief in Jesus' dignity may have co-existed. Nevertheless, on the evidence of the Fourth Gospel itself, it seems likely that the evangelist's christology is the result of a historical development, occasioned by conflicts with non-Christian Jews.

If such literary dependence or theological development can be established, it can still be asked *how much* later in time the book in question is likely to have been written. How many years must have elapsed for Mark's gospel to have acquired sufficient authority for it to have been used by the other synoptic evangelists? How long would it have taken for the Johannine community to progress from the use of titles such as are found in the vocation stories (John 1: 35-51: 'rabbi', 'Messiah', 'Son of God', 'king of Israel', 'Son of man') to the exalted christology of the prologue (1: 1-18) and the later discourses?

The expectation of Jesus' return

Another theological development which has been used to relate the New Testament writings to each other chronologically involves eschatology—the teaching concerning the end of the world. As we have seen (pp. 6-7), the Christian movement began with the expectation that the Lord would return soon, before the first generation of Christian disciples had passed away (Mark 13: 30 par.). The death of a Christian prior to this eagerly awaited event was regarded as something unnatural and explained as a punishment for sin (cf. 1 Cor. 11: 29-30). The efforts of many New Testament authors to deal with Christ's failure to return indicate a date of composition at a time when this problem had begun to be widely felt.

Mark has connected Jesus' prediction that 'there are some standing here who will not taste death before they see that the Kingdom of God has come with power' (Mark 9: 1) with the Transfiguration of Jesus (9: 2-8), in which, apparently, the reader is to see a partial and anticipatory fulfilment of the coming of the kingdom. Luke has connected the disciples' proclamation that 'the kingdom of God has come near to you' (Luke 10: 9; cf. v. 11) with the imminent arrival of 'the Lord' in the towns to which he sends them on ahead of him (10: 1).

In 2 Peter the Lord's failure to return appears as an objection used by 'scoffers' against the truth of the Christian faith: 'Where is the promise of his coming?' (3: 3-4). The author's response, that 'with the Lord one day is as a thousand years, and a thousand years as one day' (3: 8; cf. Ps. 90: 4), indicates that by the time this book was written, all hope of Christ's imminent return has been abandoned. It is significant that 2 Peter is generally regarded to be the latest book in the New Testament canon, the only work, in fact, which cannot have been written during the first century CE. This view is based not simply on the author's eschatology but also on his dependence upon the Epistle of Jude, itself a relatively late book.

Theological similarity as evidence for contemporaneity

Just as theological disparity may indicate a chronological separation between New Testament writings, so too theological similarity may indicate contemporaneity or even identity of authorship. For example, Luke-Acts and the Pastoral Epistles have similar views on christology, eschatology, and soteriology (i.e. the doctrine concerning salvation), as well as comparable attitudes towards the state and certain ethical matters. Whether or not these works were all written by the same person, their similarity of viewpoint serves to separate them from earlier writings, especially the authentic letters of Paul, whose authority is nevertheless appealed to in all these works.

The Gallio inscription

The subject matter of a New Testament book gives no indication of its date of composition. It does not follow that because Jesus' ministry preceded Paul's the gospels must therefore be earlier than the Pauline epistles. On the contrary, as noted earlier (pp. 6, 10), the seven acknowledged letters of Paul are the earliest writings in the New Testament collection. Their dating, in the 50s, depends upon the discovery at Delphi in 1905 of an inscription which mentions a Roman proconsul of Achaea named Gallio, who was in office after Claudius' twenty-sixth acclamation as 'imperator', a title originally conferred by soldiers on victorious generals. This enables us to determine the approximate date (50-1) of Paul's first visit to Corinth, during which, according to Acts 18: 12-17, he was brought before Gallio's tribunal. This date, in turn, provides us with a fixed point in relation to which the other events in Paul's life can be dated. From indications in Paul's letters of the period in his ministry during which they were written, their dates of composition can be approximately determined.

The dating of Luke-Acts

The only book in the New Testament which is explicitly concerned with the subject of Christian origins is the Acts of the Apostles. It is the companion volume to the Gospel of Luke, which the author, in his prologue to Acts, refers to as his 'earlier book' (Acts 1: 1) [author's translation]. Acts must therefore have been written some years after the composition of the gospel, which, in turn, is dated some time after its Marcan source. But the dating of Luke-Acts is also connected with the question of its authorship and with the attribution of the gospel by Irenaeus (*AH* III. 1. 1) to 'Luke, the beloved physician', mentioned in a letter attributed to Paul (Col. 4: 14).

A textual basis for the belief that Luke-Acts was written by a companion of Paul has been found in the 'we' passages, that is, those sections of the travel narrative in Acts which use the first person plural. The author of these sections, it is argued, must have accompanied the apostle at least on those journeys narrated in these passages. Since there is no stylistic difference, apart from the use of the pronoun, between these sections and the rest of the book, Lucan authorship can be extended to the whole of Acts.

Even if this argument were valid, there would be a logical leap from the 'companion of Paul' who supposedly authored Acts to the particular individual mentioned in Colossians. After all, Paul had more than one companion. But there is a much more fundamental difficulty. The presupposition of this argument, that the 'we' includes Paul and the author, is not supported by the texts. In Acts 16, where the plural pronoun first appears, Paul is mentioned separately: '[The slave girl] followed *Paul and us*' (v. 17). In chapter 20 Paul, together with seven companions mentioned by name, returns from Greece through Macedonia, 'but *we* sailed away from Philippi . . . and in five days came to *them* at Troas' (vv. 3-5). Upon Paul's arrival in Jerusalem, just before his arrest, '*Paul* went in *with us* to James' (Acts 21 : 18), and 'when *we* came to Rome, *Paul* was allowed to stay by himself, with the soldier that guarded him' (Acts 28 : 16), i.e. only Paul was under house arrest.

Therefore, whatever the sudden appearance of the first person plural may indicate, it does not mean that the author of the sections where the shift occurs is a companion of the apostle. Paul is not included in the 'we'; he is excluded. A more likely explanation for this phenomenon is suggested by the fact that, with one exception, the trip from Caesarea to Jerusalem (Acts 21: 15-18), all these passages are connected with sea voyages. The first person plural is well attested in this kind of Greek narrative, where it is used as a stylistic device to add greater vividness to the account.

Indeed, a theological comparison appears to rule out any personal or chronological proximity between the apostle and the author of the two-volume work. Paul's christology, as found in his authentic epistles, is strikingly different from that of Luke-Acts, which, in an even more significant difference, plays down the imminent expectation of Jesus' return so prominent in Paul. Furthermore, the sympathetic attitude towards natural religion expressed in the Areopagus speech (Acts 17: 22-31) clashes with the purely negative function given to it in Romans (1: 18 - 2: 16).

Most striking of all is Luke's restriction of the title 'apostle' to those who were followers of Jesus 'from the baptism of John until the day when he was taken up from us', that is, the ascension (Acts 1: 22). On this basis Paul is excluded from apostleship, and, in fact, Luke never calls him an apostle. The apparent exception in Acts 14: 4, 14 really proves the rule, since these verses refer back to the action of the Antiochene community, not the exalted Lord, in sending Paul and Barnabas on the mission (Acts 13: 1-3). Paul is an emissary of the church (cf. 2 Cor. 8: 23) but not 'an apostle of Jesus Christ', the title he regularly uses in the prescripts of his letters. These different understandings of 'apostle' will engage our attention in chapter 6 (see pp. 121-4).

From these examples it is apparent that the dating of the New Testament books is not an exact science; for this the evidence is too scanty. Arguments based upon allusions to historical events (especially those of 70 CE) and upon literary dependence or theological comparison may be persuasive, but they do not provide proof. There is a majority consensus about the dating of most books, but the question remains the subject of controversy. In the absence of totally conclusive indications, theological convictions exercise an influence, conscious or unconscious, on the view taken of this matter. It is natural that those for whom the historicity of the sacred narratives has a crucial significance for faith should argue in favour of early dating, in order to bring the New Testament books as close in time as possible to the events they relate.

The testimony of the New Testament books to their contemporary situation

The dating of the available sources, even if only probable and approximate, is essential if the historian is to use them appropriately in reconstructing the origins of the Christian movement. For the New Testament books cast light, first of all, on the period in which they were composed. The New Testament writers were not merely collectors of material. Even though, apart from Paul, their true names are no longer known, they are all authors in the proper sense, with a message for a particular individual (Luke 1: 3; Acts 1: 1; Philem. 1; 3 John 1), community (e.g. Rom. 1: 7; 1 Cor. 1: 2), or group of communities (e.g. 1 Pet. 1: 1; Rev. 1: 4). (When a book is addressed to an individual, this person may represent a wider group.) The historian listens in on the communication between the author and his addressee(s), in the hope of learning something about the historical circumstances in which this communication took place.

The influence of literary genre

How much a particular New Testament book reveals of the historical circumstances in which it was written depends in part on its literary form or genre. Apart from the one volume specifically concerned with Christian origins, the writings which are most informative about the earliest history of the movement are those whose subject matter concerns the current situation of Christian communities—the New Testament epistles. As one would expect, it is in Acts and the epistles that the church is most prominent. By contrast, the word 'church' occurs in only two verses in all four gospels (Matt. 16: 18; 18: 17).

However, just as the epistles are not concerned exclusively with the present but refer back to those past events on which the Christian faith is founded, so too, the first four books of the New Testament, the gospels, whose subject matter is the life, death, and resurrection of Jesus, cast light on the situation of the Christian communities for which they were written. For each evangelist tells the story of Jesus in such a way as to meet the current needs and problems of his community. Similarly, the Book of Revelation, though focused on the future coming of the Lord (22: 20) to rescue his persecuted followers, reveals a good deal about the Christian church in confrontation with the Roman empire and the imperial cult.

The sources of the New Testament authors

However much the New Testament writings reflect the historical situation in which they arise, none of them is simply a creation of the author. The New Testament is the primary source for the historian, but the New Testament writers had their own sources, and after the historian has learned what he can about the circumstances in which the New Testament books were written, he must go on to consider and evaluate the sources which his sources have used.

The most obvious source for the New Testament authors was the Old Testament, primarily in its Greek translation, the Septuagint. This alone was holy scripture for the first Christians, and it is another indication of the late date of 2 Peter that it implicitly refers to the letters of Paul as 'scripture' (3: 16). The New Testament authors did not view the Old Testament simply as a document from the past, nor did they experience the sense of distance from the text which a modern historical approach inevitably entails. They believed that the scriptures contained God's will for his people here and now. As Paul reminds the Romans, 'Whatever was written in former days was written for our instruction' (Rom. 15: 4).

Biblical interpretation in the first century CE

For the apostle, the story of Abraham proved that God was now offering Jew and Gentile alike the gift of righteousness through faith in Jesus Christ, apart from the works of the Mosaic law (Gal. 3: 6-18; Rom. 4: 1-25). Such an 'updating' of the Bible was not peculiar to Christian writers. Among the Qumran writings we have examples of biblical interpretation which operate on the same principle. The Pesharim or 'commentaries' study the biblical text verse by verse in order to find a meaning applicable to the past history of the sect, its present circumstances, or its future hope. The Christians and the Qumran community both appear to have made 'testimonia'—a term borrowed from the third-century writer Cyprian for collections of texts which were particularly useful in 'proving' the claims of the community in controversy with other groups.

Whatever their specific differences in interpretation, Christians and Jews had a common exegetical tradition, which is revealed most clearly in the early Targums or Aramaic paraphrases of the Hebrew Bible. Consequently the Bible used by the New Testament writers is an *interpreted* Bible. Between the Old and New Testaments lies the intermediary of Jewish tradition, in which the history of Israel, its institutions and professions of faith are treated in a manner quite different from the one used in our modern historical exegesis. Furthermore, no distinction is made between the traditional interpretation given to the scriptures in preaching and teaching and the meaning of the scriptures themselves; such a distinction would presuppose a historical consciousness which did not yet exist.

Interaction between 'prophecy' and 'fulfilment'

Since they understood the scriptures to be telling *their* story, the New Testament authors freely adapted the Old Testament text to make it conform to its 'fulfilment' in the Christian narrative, and, conversely, they adapted the Christian narrative to make it conform to the Old Testament text. An example of the former procedure is found in Matthew's citation of Isa. 7: 14 in his infancy narrative (Matt. 1: 23). The Septuagint reading of this text has 'you (i.e. King Ahaz) shall call his name Emmanuel'. Since Matthew has the angel say to Joseph 'You shall call his name *Jesus*' (1: 21), he follows a textual variant of the Isaiah citation which can be interpreted: '*they* shall call', i.e. the people whom Jesus has come to save from their sins (v. 21).

An example of the second procedure occurs in the Matthean passion story. The evangelist has (mis)interpreted the synonymous parallelism in Zech. 9: 9 ('riding on an ass, on a colt the foal of an ass') as signifying the presence of *two* animals. Accordingly, we have the curious representation of Jesus seated on both the ass and the colt: 'they brought the ass and the colt, and put their garments on them and he sat thereon' (Matt. 21: 7).

In itself, the presence of a scriptural citation does not call into question the historicity of what is reported. Although it may be disputed whether Roman law in Jesus' day prescribed that the garments of a condemned criminal should be divided among his executioners, the mere fact that the division of Jesus' clothes (Mark 15: 24) is narrated in the words of Ps. 22: 18 does not prove this detail to be a fabrication. Nevertheless, a 'fusion of horizons' results from the reciprocal influence between the Old Testament and New Testament texts, and this complicates the task of historical evaluation.

Interaction between Judaism and Hellenism

The age in which the New Testament books were written was marked by a unique cultural interaction between Hellenism and Judaism, which is expressed in the variety of sources used by the New Testament writers. These include sayings of John the Baptist (e.g. Mark 1: 8-9 par.), quotations from Greek authors such as Menander (1 Cor. 15: 33) and Aratus (Acts 17: 28), and even an allusion to the apocryphal Assumption of Moses (Jude 9). According to most scholars, one New Testament book, the gospel of Mark, has been used in the composition of two other books, the gospels of Matthew and Luke. In most instances, however, the sources of the New Testament have not been preserved. Those used by Mark and John, for example, must be reconstructed from the canonical gospels themselves.

Indications of earlier sources

Sometimes the New Testament authors make clear that they are citing an earlier source. Paul declares that he himself had received the confessional affirmations which he delivered in turn to the Corinthians when he preached the gospel to them (1 Cor. 15: 3).

But even apart from this acknowledgement, we would know that this early creed is not Paul's own formulation. The phrases 'on the third day' and 'the Twelve' do not occur elsewhere in the Pauline corpus, and the Greek verb forms rendered 'he was raised' and 'he appeared' are not found outside this chapter.

The presence of a theological conception foreign to the writer is another indication that he is using traditional material. For example, in exhorting the Philippians to humility, Paul cites a hymn which narrates the humiliation and exaltation of Christ (Phil. 2: 6-11). This theological schema contrasts with the one which Paul normally uses—Jesus' cross and resurrection. The phrase in verse 8, 'even death on a cross', disturbs the strophic structure and appears to be a Pauline addition.

Sometimes scholars have cited archaic confessional formulations as evidence for the early dating of the book in which they appear. The unusual christological titles found in Acts, e.g. 'the righteous one' (3: 14; 7: 52; 22: 14) and 'the servant of God' (3: 13, 26; 4: 27, 30) have been used in this way. However, the presence of traditional material in a New Testament book tells us nothing about the date of the book itself. The real significance of such material is in making it possible to reconstruct, at least in part, the early stages of Christian belief which preceded the more developed 'theologies' of the New Testament authors.

Stylistic assimilation and 'imitatio'

A writer can assimilate his sources to his own style and theological idiom so that they are virtually undetectable. For example, in the book of Acts everything is so 'Lucan' that no certain conclusions as to sources can be determined by stylistic analysis. Although C. C. Torrey defended the view that the first half of Acts is a literal translation of an Aramaic source, the linguistic evidence on which he based his position is better explained as Luke's conscious imitation of Septuagintal style. The old-fashioned aura of the language of the Greek Bible served to make a holy, 'apostolic' impression on the reader, much as Livy's archaic Latin style suggests the days of ancient Rome.

The sources of Acts

Although Luke must have depended on previous traditions in writing about events of which he had no personal knowledge, no attempt to identify a continuous source in the first half of Acts has won general acceptance. Once the stylistic purpose of the 'we' passages is recognized, the identification of Luke's sources for the second half of the book becomes equally problematical. Nevertheless, it is obvious from the sparseness of the narrative (e.g. 13: 4-12), the summary mode of presentation (e.g. 19: 1-12), and the gaps in the story, that the author is not relying simply on a fertile imagination. Sometimes the historian may find unintentional traces of earlier tradition in details which conflict with Luke's own perspective. For example, the fact that 'the apostles', i.e. the Twelve, were left undisturbed during the persecution of the Jerusalem church which followed the death of Stephen (Acts 8: 1) suggests that the division between the Hellenists (Greek-speaking Jewish Christians) and the Hebrews (Aramaic-speaking Jewish Christians) went beyond the daily distribution of food to the widows (Acts 6: 1), and it raises questions about the exemplary unanimity which Luke attributes to the Jerusalem community (4: 32).

The sources of the Jesus tradition

The identification and evaluation of sources becomes most sensitive and controversial in the case of the Jesus tradition. Practically speaking, the four canonical gospels are our sole access to the Jesus of history, whatever the purposes for which they were actually written. During the nineteenth century the quest for the historical Jesus coincided with the investigation of the 'synoptic problem'. As a result, interest in the 'historical Jesus' problem tended to concentrate on Mark, as the oldest of the four gospels. But the final date of composition of the other three and their dependence on Mark (which is questionable in the case of the Fourth Gospel) has little bearing on the date or historical value of the materials which they contain.

In addition to what Matthew and Luke have borrowed from Mark, they have some two hundred and thirty-five verses of discourse material not found in the earliest gospel. Such material, common to Matthew and Luke, points to a 'sayings source'—no longer extant—which either supplemented the predominantly narrative material found in Mark or else constituted an independent 'gospel' in which the interest in Jesus' death and resurrection, common to all four canonical gospels, was surprisingly absent. Furthermore, each gospel contains material not found in any other. Although such special material may have originated with the evangelist himself, it may also stem from an earlier tradition which he alone has used.

Because of its developed christology, the Fourth Gospel has been generally neglected in life of Jesus studies, a curious example of scholarly illogicality. The historian needs to sift all available materials, and at important points John contradicts the synoptic tradition. For example, in the Fourth Gospel Jesus makes several trips to Jerusalem instead of only one, and he dies on the day before Passover (John 18: 28) rather than on Passover itself (Mark 14. 12). In such cases there is no justification for dismissing *a priori* the Johannine witness.

As in the case of Acts, the Fourth Gospel exhibits a stylistic unity which discourages attempts to identify the author's sources. However, the narrative sections of the gospel exhibit many inconsistencies, awkward connections, and even contradictions which cannot be accounted for by textual criticism. A growing number of critics agree with Bultmann in explaining this literary phenomenon, which distinguishes the Fourth Gospel from the other three, by the hypothesis of a 'signs source'. The two signs performed at Cana (John 2: 11; 4: 54) seem to point to such a collection of miracle stories.

It is generally acknowledged that prior to the composition of Mark's gospel there existed written collections of related materials, for example a parable source and a collection of controversies between Jesus and the scribes. Many scholars also believe that Mark has based his 'eschatological discourse' on an apocalyptic 'pamphlet' of Jewish or Jewish-Christian origin which may have been occasioned by the plan of the Emperor Caligula to introduce into the temple a representation of himself—the 'abomination of desolation' (AV) of Mark 13: 14. The parenthetical admonition, 'Let the reader understand', seems out of place in what, ostensibly, is a spoken discourse (Mark 13: 5) and points to a written source.

But attention has focused mainly on the individual 'pericopes' (short, self-contained units of tradition) which, with the notable exception of the passion story, make up the narrative material in the synoptic tradition. Ever since the study by K. L. Schmidt, it has been generally recognized that 'the framework of the (synoptic) gospels' is the redactional contribution of the first evangelist, Mark. It does not preserve a historical recollection of the sequence of events in Jesus' ministry. Not only did the later evangelists feel free to depart from Mark's order at a number of points. In Mark's gospel itself the way in which the individual stories are linked together is quite artificial. This can be illustrated by the sequence in which we find the call of the first disciples (Mark 1: 16-20) and Jesus in the synagogue at Capharnaum on the sabbath (Mark 1: 21-8). Since the second scene follows 'immediately' (v. 21) upon the first, one might conclude that the sons of Zebedee were breaking the law in mending their nets (v. 19) on the sabbath (v. 21). Since this inference is clearly not intended by the evangelist, the connection between the two pericopes must be literary and not chronological.

Once the redactional links have been severed, the units of tradition can be studied individually, like pearls from which the connecting string has been removed. The evaluation of these pre-gospel units is one of the most controversial questions in New Testament scholarship today, and it is of crucial importance for the historian to consider how this material originated and how it was shaped and transmitted until it reached the form in which we have it.

A study of the pre-history of the synoptic tradition involves the crucial transition from the oral to the written stage. Today we can no longer assume a simple continuity between the oral traditions and the written end product. The fixity of the written word contrasts with the phase of oral transmission, where each spoken delivery is a fresh creative act. The failure to recognize the uniqueness of the written text is a major shortcoming in the two principal models which have been developed to study the pre-gospel tradition.

Form criticism

Form criticism, the first model which we shall consider, applied to the synoptic tradition the methods devised by the Old Testament scholar, Hermann Gunkel, for studying the individual stories incorporated in the sources of the Pentateuch. Like its Old Testament counterpart, New Testament form criticism was an attempt to go beyond the results of source criticism. The two leading practitioners of the method were Martin Dibelius and Rudolf Bultmann. Dibelius was mainly concerned with narrative, whereas Bultmann analysed the entire synoptic tradition, under the two general divisions of narrative and discourse.

Both scholars classify their material according to a variety of 'forms', although they differ in their terminology for them. Both agree that a 'form' is neither something accidental nor the result of the literary genius of an individual. Rather, it is the spontaneous creation of a community and grows out of a typical, recurring situation in the life of the community, such as preaching, teaching, or controversy with outsiders. By observing the laws which govern the transmission of the material, as illustrated by different synoptic accounts of the same story, the form critics attempt to reconstruct the history of each form (*Formgeschichte*), working backwards from its earliest *written* version in the gospel, in order to arrive at the earliest recoverable level of the community tradition.

Since, according to the theory of form criticism, each form is a function of the life of the community, a study of the forms of the gospel tradition reveals the concerns of the community which brought them into being. In other words, the thrust of form criticism is sociological. It sheds light on what is typical in the life of the Christian community, not on particular occurrences, whether in the life of the community or in the life of Jesus.

Bultmann is explicit on this point. He suggests that the title of his book *Jesus* could be put in quotation marks. For it is not Jesus himself but 'the complex of thoughts present in the oldest level of the tradition which is the subject of our investigation'. Although the community tradition which has attained written form in the synoptic gospels *presupposes* the preaching of Jesus, form criticism is unable to determine whether or not the earliest level of this tradition actually goes back to Jesus.

For the historian, acceptance of the presuppositions of form criticism would entail abandoning Jesus as a possible subject for investigation. For the theologian, it would mean reducing Jesus, who is the subject of the church's proclamation, to a mere name or cipher, with the consequent danger that this proclamation, being deprived of all historical content, could become a sort of myth. It is this consequence which led some of Bultmann's own students to try to get 'behind' the earliest community tradition to Jesus himself.

A basis for doing this seemed available in the 'criterion of dissimilarity'. Anything in the earliest level of community tradition which had no parallel either in contemporary Judaism or in the post-Easter Christian church could be attributed to Jesus. There are serious difficulties with this attempt to mitigate the radical consequences of form criticism, and it is significant that Bultmann himself did not respond to it positively. It would be a rash scholar who would state categorically that something in the gospel tradition had no parallel in first century Judaism. Given the limitations of our knowledge, the absence of a particular conception in the Jewish sources is scarcely conclusive. Moreover, since the dating of Jewish tradition is a difficult problem, it is not always possible to say how much material in Jewish sources goes back to the first century CE.

There are equal difficulties with the second half of the criterion of dissimilarity. If something in the gospel tradition has no parallel in Christian tradition, it may be said to represent pre-Easter tradition, but from this it does not follow that it derives from Jesus. Although the form critics set the beginning of the gospel tradition at Easter, this is actually quite arbitrary. During his ministry Jesus was surrounded by a group of disciples who made up a community in which certain typical situations recurred. Such a community fulfils the requirements of the form critics for the formation of tradition. But though the origins of gospel tradition may lie in the pre-Easter period, it is impossible to establish that this earliest tradition goes back to Jesus, once one has accepted the premisses of form criticism. From a sociological datum it is impossible to infer an individual point of origin.

Finally, there is a theological presupposition in assuming that whatever is 'unique' in the gospel tradition must come from Jesus. From the fact that something is without parallel in either Judaism or Christianity, the strict conclusion is simply that its source is as yet

unknown. Even if the historian were to judge that the material is
original, it does not follow automatically that it goes back to Jesus.
We may legitimately assume that there was something about Jesus
which explains how he came to be the object of the church's preaching, but we cannot postulate that this quality expressed itself in
words or deeds for which there are no historical parallels. Even the
greatest teachers often say and do familiar things.

Besides such dubious attempts at revisionism by scholars who
basically accept form criticism, direct challenges have been addressed
to the presuppositions of the method. In particular, the attempt to
explain the origins of the synoptic material by the collective creativity
of a community rests upon an unproven assumption. No evidence
for such spontaneous creativity is offered from studies of oral cul-
tures, and it seems that the form critics adopted a romantic view of
'folk' culture which is rejected by contemporary sociologists. Though
the gospels themselves bear witness to the 'updating' of earlier
tradition to make it speak to contemporary needs, such shaping of
tradition is quite a different thing from creating it. Moreover,
stereotyped patterns of narration may depend more on what is being
narrated than on recurring situations in the life of the community.
Healings, for example, are described in the same way because,
generally speaking, they take place in the same way.

It is significant that form criticism has rarely won unqualified
acceptance outside the German-speaking area, and today German
scholars are included among those who maintain that the method
has not lived up to its promising beginnings. Vincent Taylor, one of
the first British scholars to evaluate the works of Bultmann and
Dibelius, welcomed the study of the narrative forms used in popular
tradition, but he cautioned against expecting such study to solve the
problem of gospel origins. Formal classifications cannot answer
historical questions, and the historian is more impressed by probable
explanations than by hypothetical constructs and inexorable laws of
oral transmission. This is particularly the case when a study of the
synoptic gospels discloses the operation of contradictory tendencies
in the development of tradition, for example, both a tendency
towards simplification and a tendency to add details not present in
the earlier version. As for the idea of 'collective creativity', Dennis

Nineham, though more open than Taylor to the influence of the community in shaping the tradition, took for granted that its origins lie in eye-witness testimony, however little expression of this may be found in our gospel narratives.

A Scandinavian alternative

A vastly different model for the origin and transmission of the gospel tradition is offered by a Swedish scholar, Harald Riesenfeld, and his student, Birger Gerhardsson. In their view, the primary situation within the community for the transmission of the Jesus tradition is tradition itself, that is, tradition as a conscious technical act of instruction. This Scandinavian approach has an advantage over form criticism in being based on a historical analogy, rather than on the romantic idea of the creative community. This analogy is the transmission of the oral torah in rabbinic Judaism. Gerhardsson's solution to the problem of the formation of the gospel tradition follows the Scandinavian 'traditio-historical' approach used in Old Testament research, just as Bultmann and Dibelius adopted the form critical method of the German Old Testament scholar, Gunkel.

In rabbinic Judaism there existed a methodical, controlled transmission of 'the tradition of the Fathers', which Gerhardsson sees paralleled in 'the ministry of the word' exercised by the Twelve in Jerusalem (Acts 6: 4). Like the Jewish 'traditionists' (*tannā'îm*), a group of official repeaters, 'the ministers of the word' (Luke 1: 2) were responsible for the verbatim transmission of oral passages. The statement which Paul makes, both about the early creed (1 Cor. 15: 3) and the Lord's supper (1 Cor. 11: 23), that he 'delivered' to the Corinthians what he himself had 'received', parallels the technical terminology used for the controlled transmission of the oral torah. The division of the gospel tradition into discourse and narrative parallels the two sources of the oral torah, namely, the sayings of the great rabbis and their deeds.

It is significant that Gerhardsson's argument depends more on Paul and Acts than on the gospels themselves. To establish his thesis that the Jesus tradition in the gospels is the result of controlled verbatim transmission, Gerhardsson is obliged to rely on patristic statements. But the concern of the post-apostolic church to connect the New Testament books, especially the gospels, with apostolic authorities says more about the needs of the church during this later period than it does about the historical origins of the books themselves.

The rise of historical consciousness, already present in Luke-Acts, brings with it the problem of the connection with one's origins, and it is this problem which the post-apostolic church endeavours to solve by regarding the canonical gospels as 'apostolic writings' authored by two of the Twelve (Matthew and John) and two disciples of apostles (Mark, the disciple of Peter, and Luke, the disciple of Paul). There is no conclusive evidence in the gospels themselves either of apostolic authorship or of the kind of systematic, word for word traditioning which Gerhardsson postulates.

On the contrary, the extraordinary freedom with which the Jesus tradition was transmitted has resulted in divergent versions even of such fundamental sayings as the Lord's Prayer (Matt. 6: 9-13 par.) and the words of institution (Mark 14: 22-5 par.). This diversity calls into question the suitability of the rabbinic analogy. Christianity is a historical religion in the sense that its fundamental faith affirmations are in the past tense, but the early church's fervent expectation of the Lord's imminent return and its conviction that its actions were under the guidance of Christ's spirit resulted in a view of its past and a use of its tradition which were quite different from what we find in Judaism. Moreover, Gerhardsson presupposes the existence in the first Christian century of techniques which are not attested until second-century Judaism. The conservatism reflected in the transmission of Jewish oral tradition may be a reaction against the charismatic, apocalyptic, enthusiasm of the Christian movement.

The gospels in the context of Graeco-Roman literature

Although the form critical and Scandinavian approaches have both made significant contributions, neither provides the historian with a reliable model for evaluating the Jesus tradition. Thanks to increased co-operation between New Testament and classics scholars, the study of the gospels is now being integrated into the study of Graeco-Roman literature. When seen against this background, some of the characteristics of the gospels no longer appear quite so distinctive, and the historical problems of the Jesus tradition no longer exceed the problems which, as we have seen, confront any student of ancient history.

It is often stated that form criticism has demonstrated that the gospels are not what the ordinary reader would take them to be, biographies or lives of Jesus. Of course, the gospels cannot be compared with *modern* biographies, since modern historiography, with its emphasis on the impartial evaluation of evidence, is a product of the nineteenth century. There are relatively few biographies from the period in which the gospels were written which show an interest in chronology and the evaluation of conflicting evidence.

Except for biographical satires, most Graeco-Roman biographies are didactic in intent. A life story is narrated in order to make a moral point and to inspire the reader to imitation. The writer sees in his subject the embodiment of values which claim his personal commitment and which he hopes to communicate to the reader. This is quite in keeping with the 'kerygmatic' character of the gospels, which give more attention to the meaning of Jesus' life and death than to external events of his career and which seek to win over the reader to Christian discipleship or confirm him in the commitment which he has already made.

Though the artificial links in Mark's gospel reflect his sources, which consisted principally in unconnected pericopes, they are paralleled in Graeco-Roman biographers, who string together typical anecdotes in order to illustrate their subject's character and destiny. The ancient world did not have our modern interest in the psychological development of famous men and women. The subject appears at the beginning as a fully developed personality; anecdotes about his early years simply illustrate what he is destined to become.

From this perspective we can better appreciate the gospel 'infancy narratives'. Although Christian piety has attributed them to 'family tradition', preserved by Joseph (in Matthew) and Mary (in Luke), the numerous contradictions between the two accounts and the small amount of common material make it quite incredible that they should represent the same events as recalled by husband and wife. Rather, they are 'mini-gospels' which look both forward and backward. They anticipate the portrayal of Jesus which the evangelists will develop in the body of their works, and at the same time they form a transition between Old Testament history and the gospel story of the ministry. To readers steeped in biblical tradition, the accounts of Jesus' origins recalled the great figures of Israel's past, whose conception and birth were also accompanied by marvellous happenings.

The absence of a psychological dimension is also evident in the representation of Jesus' adult life. Albert Schweitzer used the gospels to compose a psychodrama, in which Jesus' Galilean ministry and his provocation of a violent death in Jerusalem are both motivated by a desire to bring about the coming of the kingdom. Despite the fascination of such a reconstruction, it represents a blind alley for the historian. The evangelists were concerned to show that Jesus' life and death were in conformity with God's will, as contained in the scriptures, but the human motivation behind the crucial events in the narrative is rarely explained satisfactorily. Without a continuous source for Jesus' ministry, the evangelists could not have traced his inner development, even if they had wanted to do so.

Another characteristic of the gospels which has been thought to disqualify them as historical sources is their supernaturalism—God and other supernatural beings represented as intervening directly in human affairs. But this openness to the miraculous, which separates the gospels from *modern* biographies, connects them with contemporary Graeco-Roman biographies, particularly those of the romantic genre.

Perhaps the most significant case in point is the gospel of Luke, since the author shows his familiarity with secular writers of the period in certain expressions in his prologue. In this gospel Jesus' birth is prefaced with a miraculous conception (Luke 1: 35), and the work concludes with his ascension into heaven (24: 51). Ancient lives of historical figures such as Alexander the Great and the emperor Augustus show a similar pattern: a virtuous life framed by a supernatural begetting and an apotheosis.

The Christian apologist Justin was quite aware of such similarities between the gospels and non-Christian biographies: for him the fictions of the pagans were diabolic counterfeits of Christian realities

(*Dialogue with Trypho* 69, 70; 1 *Apology* 54). Modern rationalists use such similarities to support the thesis that the gospels are imitations of pagan myths. Neither explanation is verifiable by historical means. Our concern is rather to suggest that the extreme historical scepticism of some New Testament scholars may be the result of studying the gospels in isolation from contemporary writings of the same genre.

Apart from Cicero and Caesar, there is probably no figure in antiquity whose life can be documented in the way which modern standards require. Nevertheless, 'biographies' of ancient personages —Jesus included—continue to be written. Rather than retreat into an unrealistic hypercriticism, the student of the New Testament should consider by what methods the available sources can best be used to reconstruct the life of Jesus.

3

Jesus of Nazareth

The most obvious unifying element in the New Testament writings is their common concern for Jesus Christ. It is therefore impossible to write about the origins of Christianity without including a chapter on the person to whom the earliest Christian community believed it owed its existence. Jesus of Nazareth is also the historical link between Judaism and Christianity. To be sure, it was only in the latter decades of the first century that Christians began to perceive themselves as a religious movement distinct from Judaism. Moreover, their sense of separation from the parent faith may have had as much to do with the changing ethnic composition of the community as with theological matters. Luke connects the use of the term 'Christian' with Antioch (Acts 11: 26), where missionaries from Cyprus and Cyrene 'spoke to the Greeks also [i.e. non-Jews], preaching the Lord Jesus' (v. 20).

Nevertheless, 'preaching the Lord Jesus' was undoubtedly the principal characteristic of the new Jewish sect from its beginning. It was this which led 'Christian' Jews—the adjective, though anachronistic, is necessary for clarity—to regard themselves as Jews of a special kind, indeed as 'a remnant, chosen by grace' (Rom. 11: 5) from 'a disobedient and contrary people' (Rom. 10: 21 = Isa. 65: 2). Convictions about the significance of Jesus, not differences concerning the interpretation of the law (as in the case of Qumran), distinguished Christians from other Jews.

Before the Jewish War, Christians who observed the law could co-exist with other Jews as one group among many. After 70 CE, however, their belief in Jesus as the Christ caused them to be treated as heretics by normative Judaism. The person of Jesus was therefore central both to Christians' understanding of themselves in their difference from other Jews and to Jewish attitudes towards Christians, especially after the war. Once the separation between church and synagogue had occurred, Jesus the Jew was a continual, if unwelcome, reminder to Jews and Christians of the Jewish origins of the Christian movement.

Jesus as a historical problem

It is ironic that this pivotal position of Jesus in religious history has led to such difficulties in the historical investigation of Jesus himself. Some scholars have insisted that the early church has incorporated Jewish teaching, as well as its own 'Christian' teaching, into the gospels (see p. 38). As a result, it is often argued, only gospel material which has no parallel either in first-century Judaism or in early Christianity can be considered 'authentic', that is, as coming from Jesus himself. Apart from the difficulty of implementing this 'criterion of dissimilarity', it betrays an approach to the data which the historian is reluctant to accept. At best, its results lead to a distorted picture: what *distinguishes* Jesus from the religion to which he belonged and the religion which stemmed from him cannot tell us what was *characteristic* about him or enable us to grasp him as a historical personality. For this the material in the shaded areas of the diagram must be included.

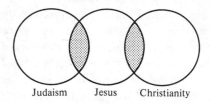

Judaism   Jesus   Christianity

Theological presuppositions of the 'new quest'

The minimalism and scepticism of the 'new quest' for the historical Jesus stems from the theological postulates of Bultmann's school, to which most of these scholars belong. Bultmann's fear that fallible judgements about history might be made the basis for faith has no legitimate bearing on the conduct of historical inquiry, and the criterion of dissimilarity does not assist the investigation of the Jesus tradition. Since the historian claims nothing beyond probability for his reconstruction, he will prefer to make use of all material which is probably authentic, rather than to exclude what is possibly inauthentic, particularly if the reasons advanced for inauthenticity are themselves improbable.

Since Jesus was a Jew, it is not surprising that some of his sayings and parables have Jewish parallels. Unless some plausible reason can be given why the Christian community should attribute such material to him, it seems reasonable to suppose that Jesus is drawing on Jewish tradition. The crucial question of the burden of proof—for or against authenticity—will be viewed differently by the historian and by the type of theologian who insists on absolute certitude.

Two theories of post-Easter creation of gospel tradition

It has been suggested that the gospel controversies between Jesus and his opponents arose out of debates within the Christian community. This theory is quite unproven and has little to commend it. Of course, the community would turn to their remembrance of what Jesus had said and done in attempting to resolve contemporary problems. Such concerns would have determined which traditions about Jesus were preserved. However, these gospel stories reflect Jesus' own time and situation, not the time and situation of the early church, and therefore they cannot be early Christian inventions. Bultmann sees the 'life situation' for such controversies in the community debates attested in the rabbinic tradition, but there is no evidence that such debates were actually carried on in Christian communities.

Equally untenable is the theory which explains Jesus' sayings in the gospels as the inspired utterances of early Christian prophets. There are instances where sayings are attributed to the *risen* Jesus or the spirit, but where this occurs, it is usually clear from the context. In Matt. 28: 19 a saying is placed on the lips of the exalted Lord which endorses the Gentile mission, an issue which did not arise during Jesus' own lifetime. In Jesus' grant of ecclesiastical authority to Peter (Matt. 16: 17-19), the post-resurrectional character of the saying is indicated by the phrase 'flesh and blood has not revealed this to you' (v. 17). Paul uses similar language in speaking of his experience of the risen Lord (Gal. 1: 16).

In Revelation the saying of the Son of man (1: 13), 'Lo, I am coming like a thief!' (16: 15), is reported by John (1: 9) while 'in the spirit' (v. 10), which makes clear the charismatic nature of the communication. The appointment of Saul and Barnabas for the mission (Acts 13: 2) is attributed to 'the holy spirit', and the presence of prophets (v. 1) indicates the medium of communication. However, the eschatological instructions which Paul ascribes to 'the word of the Lord' (1 Thess. 4: 15) could derive from something in Jesus' preaching which has not otherwise been preserved (cf. Acts 20: 35), as well as from some special prophetic revelation.

Although early Christian communities appealed to the ecstatic utterances of prophets (2 Thess. 2: 2), there is simply no evidence that such sayings were routinely attributed to the earthly Jesus and thus found their way into the gospels. When neither the content nor the context indicates a situation after Easter, the inauthenticity of sayings attributed to Jesus in the gospels must be proved, not assumed. To operate on any other basis would restrict the historian's use of material in a way which no sound methodology can justify.

Jesus' condemnation and death: the starting point for historical reconstruction

The reconstruction of Jesus' life and teaching starts with the indisputable fact of his death on the cross. From this event we work backwards to the collapse of his movement for a national religious revival and to his conflict with Jewish religious leaders, which dashed the hopeful beginnings of his ministry. Jesus' mode of execution leaves no doubt that the responsibility for his death lay with the Roman prefect of Judaea, Pontius Pilate. The charge on which he was condemned was affixed to his cross, as all four evangelists report (Mark 15: 26 par.). Whether or not Jesus himself had claimed to be 'the king of the Jews' (cf. John 19: 21), Pilate considered him to be, at least potentially, a threat to the stability of Roman rule.

It is not necessary to believe that Jesus was a Zealot (a Jew committed to the expulsion of the Romans by force of arms) or even sympathetic to the Zealot cause. Apart from the fact that one of his followers had belonged to this movement (Mark 3: 18 par.), no evidence can be cited in support of this hypothesis, apart from the obscure saying in Luke 22: 36, and the use of violence contradicts Jesus' explicit teaching on the love of enemies (Luke 6: 27-36 par.). Furthermore, the fact that Jesus alone was arrested rules out the view that he intended to spark an uprising against the Romans (cf. John 18: 36). However, the crowd's acclamation of Jesus as he entered the holy city (Mark 11: 9 par.) and his own claim to authority (Mark 11: 28 par.) in driving the money-changers out of the temple (Mark 11: 15-17 par.) could be used to make a *prima facie* case against him, and Pilate was not hesitant to take drastic action in such a situation, especially when a Galilean was involved (cf. Luke 13: 1).

There is an evident tendency in the gospels to obscure Roman responsibility for Jesus' death. Luke has Pilate repeatedly declare Jesus' innocence (Luke 23: 4, 14, 22), and in Matthew's gospel Pilate washes his hands before the crowd as he proclaims his innocence in Jesus' death (Matt. 27: 24). In the Fourth Gospel Pilate actually hands Jesus over to the high-priests to be crucified (John 19: 16). This development in the gospel tradition is explained both by the hostility of the Christian community towards the Jewish authorities and by its need to win political toleration from the Roman authorities. The fact that Jesus had been put to death as 'the king of the Jews' suggested that the movement which stemmed from him might pose a danger to the state, and this suspicion could have serious consequences for Christians.

On the other hand, Roman responsibility does not exclude Jewish complicity. The Sanhedrin included scribes, who would not have forgotten Jesus' opposition to the Pharisees during his ministry. The Sadducees may have been genuinely apprehensive that Jesus' popularity with the masses could provoke Roman intervention (John 11: 47-50). It is therefore entirely plausible that the Jewish leaders in Jerusalem facilitated Jesus' condemnation by Pilate or even took the initiative, as the gospels suggest. In John 18: 31 they declare, 'It is not lawful for us to put anyone to death', and no conclusive evidence to the contrary has yet been adduced. If Jesus was to be done away with, he had to be condemned to death by the Romans, and that could only be done on the basis of a political, not a religious, charge.

However, what we know about Pilate from extra-biblical sources does not confirm the gospel picture of a weak man who desired to save Jesus' life but was overwhelmed by pressure from the Jewish leaders. On the contrary, he seems to have been a cruel and ruthless ruler, who had nothing but contempt for the people under his authority. It has been suggested that, in view of the situation at Tiberius' court, the implicit threat to denounce Pilate in Rome for not being 'Caesar's friend' (John 19: 12) could have been an effective means of intimidation. However, the need to make such a threat presupposes that Pilate was actually trying to have Jesus released, as the gospel affirms, and this is the very point in doubt.

A comparative study of the four passion accounts reveals numerous divergences, which cannot be discussed here. Scholarly opinion on the antiquity of the traditions behind this section of the gospels is divided. The views range from the suggestion that Mark was the first to redact a continuous passion story to the hypothesis of a lengthy pre-Marcan narrative, beginning in Mark 8: 27 with the episode at Caesarea Philippi. A middle position affirms the existence of a pre-Marcan narrative which began with the arrest of Jesus and included his appearance before the Sanhedrin, a trial by Pilate, Jesus' condemnation and way of the cross, and his crucifixion and death. Although theological reflection has already left its mark on this primitive account, its significance for the historian should not be underrated.

The episode which has occasioned the most debate is undoubtedly Jesus' appearance before the Sanhedrin (Mark 14: 53, 55-65). According to the Lucan (Luke 22: 66-71) and Johannine (John 18: 13, 19-24) parallels, the measures taken on the Jewish side did not include either a formal trial or a death sentence. Mark's account of a night trial, followed by another one in the morning (15: 1), seems unlikely, and Jewish scholars have pointed out that the proceedings of the Sanhedrin, as reported by Mark, violate the laws of the Mishnah on numerous counts. Whether these laws were already in effect in Jesus' day is disputed.

On the whole, therefore, the evidence seems to suggest that Jewish judicial involvement took the form of a preliminary investigation. Mark's information, including Jesus' alleged statement about the temple (Mark 14: 58), the question of his messiahship (vv. 61-2), and the charge of blasphemy (v. 64) were probably not part of the primitive passion narrative. However, it does not follow that these elements are simply unhistorical inventions.

Jesus is reported to have predicted the temple's destruction (Mark 13: 2), and his ministry seems to have aroused messianic expectations among the people (John 6: 15). Already in the period of the first temple the priests and court prophets had declared that Jeremiah's prophecy of the temple's destruction (Jer. 26: 6) was worthy of death (v. 11). While it is true that would-be messiahs with nationalistic aspirations were tolerated and even supported by Jewish religious authorities during the first and second centuries CE, religious opposition to someone who attacked the temple would only be strengthened by his being acclaimed as the Messiah (cf. Mark 11: 9-10 par.).

The priestly aristocracy in Jerusalem probably regarded Jesus as a false prophet (cf. Mark 14: 65 par.) who was leading Israel astray (cf. Deut. 13: 1-5). Against such a deceiver (cf. Matt. 27: 63) a charge of blasphemy would have been appropriate. Mark, or traditions on which he depended, has probably gathered together charges made against Jesus during his ministry and introduced them into the account of his appearance before the Sanhedrin, giving it the character of a formal trial.

Jesus' controversies with the scribes

There is a striking anticipation of the passion motif early in Mark's gospel: 'The Pharisees went out, and immediately held counsel with the Herodians against [Jesus], how to destroy him' (Mark 3: 6, cf. 11: 18a). This verse, which occurs at the conclusion of five controversies between Jesus and 'the scribes of the Pharisees' (Mark 2: 16), suggests a biographical concern. If it comes from the pen of the evangelist, it indicates why he includes these controversies: they explain the antipathy towards Jesus from one part of the Jewish leadership, which would play an important role in events in Jerusalem narrated later in the gospel. If the verse comes from a pre-Marcan source, it suggests that these five controversies were collected in order to explain this antipathy. In either case, Mark 2: 1 - 3: 6 would contain valuable information on points of difference between Jesus and the Pharisaic Judaism of his day.

The problem of the origin of the Jesus tradition

Scholars who insist that large parts of the Jesus tradition were radically reinterpreted or 'invented' in the post-Easter church find such an interpretation simplistic. For them these discourses represent not the recollection of historical controversies between Jesus and his theological opponents but rather disputes within the post-Easter community concerning, in particular, the observance of Sunday (cf. Rev. 1: 10; 1 Cor. 16: 2) in place of the Jewish sabbath. Since the appeal to Jesus' authority (Mark 2: 28) would obviously carry no weight with Jewish opponents, the participants in the debate are thought to be Gentile and Jewish Christians.

In such a reconstruction the plot of the Pharisees and Herodians against Jesus' life would not be a historical reminiscence. Rather, it would reflect the period following the destruction of Jerusalem, when the Pharisaic party—more specifically, those Pharisees who repudiated the revolutionary aspirations of the Zealots—became the authoritative leadership in Judaism. Such Pharisees were the only Jewish group which enjoyed Roman toleration after the cessation of the temple cult and the disappearance of the Sadducean priesthood. It was with this group that Christian Jews came into conflict in the period after 70. If interpreted against this historical background, Mark 3: 6 would be placing the blame for Jesus' death on the same group from which the Christian community was experiencing persecution (cf. Matt. 23: 34), and the Herodians could then be identified with followers of Agrippa I (41-4 CE).

Such an explanation becomes unnecessary if we take the common-sense position that the basic stimulus behind the rise of the Jesus tradition was Jesus himself. Although the first canonical gospel was not written until about forty years after Jesus' death, the church's missionary preaching kept the Jesus tradition alive. Two of the missionary sermons in Acts include a summary of Jesus' ministry. In Peter's Pentecost sermon Jesus of Nazareth is described as 'a man attested to you by God with mighty works and wonders and signs which God did through him in your midst, as you yourselves know' (Acts 2: 22). In his sermon in Cornelius' house Peter declares:

> You know the word which [God] sent to Israel, preaching good news of peace by Jesus Christ . . . the word which was proclaimed throughout all Judaea, beginning from Galilee after the baptism which John preached: how God anointed Jesus of Nazareth with the Holy Spirit and with power; how he went about doing good and healing all that were oppressed by the devil, for God was with him. (Acts 10: 36-8)

We cannot be sure to what extent Luke's sermons in Acts reflect the primitive preaching of the Jerusalem community. Nevertheless, such references to Jesus' ministry must surely have been included in the Easter proclamation, since a declaration that God had raised Jesus from the dead would have had no meaning apart from some knowledge of who Jesus was. Bultmann's view that the primitive preaching included nothing but Jesus' crucifixion and resurrection is the expression of a modern theological position; it is not a plausible historical hypothesis.

The apostle Paul, who was converted several years after Jesus' death (cf. 1 Cor. 15: 8) and fiercely proclaimed the independence of his gospel from any human authority (Gal. 1: 1, 11), shows his dependence on traditions about Jesus (1 Cor. 11: 23-5; cf. Luke 22: 19-20; 1 Cor. 15: 3 ff). He also appeals to the authority of 'the Lord' in support of certain instructions he gives the Corinthian community (1 Cor. 7: 10; cf. Mark 10: 11 par.; 1 Cor. 9: 14; cf. Luke 10: 7; Mark 2: 25-6). Paul's missionary preaching, which is presupposed in his letters to the communities he founded (cf. 1 Cor. 15: 1), probably made greater use of the Jesus tradition, with which he presumably became familiar through his interrogation of Peter during the first visit to Jerusalem after his conversion (Gal. 1: 18). In any case, his affirmation that 'no one speaking by the spirit of

God ever says, 'Jesus be cursed' (1 Cor. 12: 3) makes clear that his proclamation of the risen Christ ('Jesus is Lord') did not ignore the historical figure of Jesus of Nazareth. For Paul, as for other Christian missionaries, the recollection of Jesus' life and teaching was an integral part of the evangelistic preaching. (See J. A. Ziesler, *Pauline Christianity*, in this series, for a fuller discussion.)

The literary crystallization of the Jesus tradition did not begin to take place until several decades after the gospel was first proclaimed. Nevertheless, the canonical gospels do not present us with a transformation of the *kerygma* into fictitious narratives and sayings. Of course, the modern historian must be critical in his use of these writings. Sometimes they show a strikingly creative interpretation of the Jesus tradition (e.g. Matt. 4: 1-11 par.); some of Jesus' sayings may have been misunderstood in the process of transmission, whether through a shift in context or because of contemporary interests or dogmatic positions; at times the glory of the risen Lord breaks through the representation of Jesus' ministry (e.g. Mark 9: 2-8 par.).

Nevertheless, the gospels were written with the intention of mediating an encounter between the reader and Jesus of Nazareth. Subject to appropriate safeguards, the modern historian is entitled to use the gospels in reconstructing the life and teaching of Jesus, because he shares the evangelists' interest in the past, even though his own task does not include their concern for religious conversion.

Jesus' claim of authority

The plot on Jesus' life (Mark 3: 6) follows immediately upon two sabbath controversies. Such disputes are found in all the gospels, including John. Indeed, the Johannine evidence is especially interesting, since the sabbath references in the healing of the paralytic (John 5: 9) and of the man born blind (9: 14) merely serve to spark off the controversies which follow. The fact that Jesus healed on the sabbath is taken for granted. The pervasive recollection that such actions occurred and provoked opposition must be taken seriously by the historian.

It is less obvious on what basis Jesus justified these sabbath violations. Indeed, in the first sabbath controversy, the very nature of the violation is unclear: was it journeying on the sabbath ('the disciples made their way') or 'plucking ears of grain' (Mark 2: 23)? In any case, Jesus assumes responsibility for the behaviour of his disciples, citing the precedent of David, who made provision for 'those who were with him' (v. 26). But what does the situation of Jesus and his disciples have in common with that of David and his companions, apart from the illegality (vv. 24, 26) of the actions in question? The Pharisees acknowledged that the sabbath could be broken to save human life. Is Jesus simply taking a more 'liberal' position by extending this principle to cover the situation of hunger (v. 25), even when there is no danger of death?

It has been suggested that the point of Jesus' answer is to be found in the claim of authority which it implies. For in permitting —and thus authorizing—his disciples' behaviour, Jesus compares his action with the action of David, the elect of God. In the gospel story David's companions (1 Sam. 21: 2) have a counterpart in the disciples. The responsibility for the illegal action of eating the bread of the presence is transferred from the priest Ahimelek (1 Sam. 21: 1), who becomes 'Abiathar' in the Marcan story (2: 26), to David himself: 'he entered the house of God . . ., ate the bread of the presence . . ., and also gave it to those who were with him' (v. 26).

The issue of authority becomes explicit in the closing verses of this pericope. Since Jesus' answer to the Pharisees has already been given in vv. 25-6, it seems likely that vv. 27-8 are either taken from another sabbath controversy or else constitute a separate instruction of the disciples. Here again, it is not a question of Jesus taking a 'liberal' position, as v. 27, taken by itself, might suggest. In Jewish tradition Mattathias, the father of the five Maccabee brothers, is credited with the saying: 'The sabbath has been given over to you, but you have not been given over to the sabbath' (Mekh. Exod. 31, 14). Against the background of 1 Macc. 2, the saying refers to the decision that the resistance fighters may defend themselves, if they are attacked on the sabbath (v. 41).

Jesus' use of the principle is quite different. Although in the Greek New Testament 'Son of man' has become a christological title —an expression of Jesus' dignity—the original Aramaic phrase seems to have been used as a means of veiled self-designation. In Mark 2: 28, therefore, Jesus connects the general statement that 'the sabbath was made for man' with the authority which *he*—not his Pharisaic opponents—possesses as 'lord of the sabbath'. He has the right to determine how the sabbath can be made to serve the beneficient purpose for which God instituted it.

Without an implicit reference to Jesus' authority, his rhetorical question in Mark 3: 4 fails to justify the sabbath violation in the healing of the man with the withered hand (Mark 3: 1-6). Since the man was not in any danger of death, Jesus' desire 'to do good' did not have to be carried out on the sabbath (cf. Luke 13: 14). But Jesus did not consider his healing ministry to be on a par with the activity of other miracle workers, of which he was quite aware (cf. Matt. 12: 27 par.). His ministry was the unique expression of God's own saving activity (cf. John 5: 17) and, as such, took precedence over the sabbath law even in a non-urgent situation.

Jesus' conflicts with the religious leaders of his day involved the two most sacred institutions of Judaism: the temple and the sabbath. In the matter of sabbath observance Jesus was not a liberal, proclaiming that human comfort and convenience take precedence over God's law. Nor was he a casuist, who simply extended the legal principle of excusing causes further than his Pharisaic opponents would allow. Rather, Jesus claimed the right to decide specific questions of sabbath observance on his own authority, an authority which he believed to be rooted in his mission from God.

Jesus' understanding of his mission

The historian can pass no judgement on the validity or legitimacy of Jesus' sense of mission. Nevertheless, he is entitled to affirm its existence on the basis of sayings in which Jesus defends himself and his disciples against hostile accusations. Whatever the differences between Jesus and the Pharisees in the observance of the sabbath, a plausible explanation for their intense opposition to him must include his justification of his practice.

In the religion of Jesus' day, centuries after the last of the prophets, authority was located in the scriptures and the scribal interpretations given to them. Jesus' teaching and behaviour were

rooted in a personal authority which impressed itself on those who
came in contact with him (cf. Mark 1: 22; John 7: 46), whether they
were favourably disposed towards him or not. The contention of the
form critics that all gospel sayings which express Jesus' authority are
creations of the post-Easter faith 'explains' the data by appealing to
something which is itself in need of explanation. To the historian
Jesus' assessment of himself and his ministry and the impact of this
self-understanding on others are important for explaining both the
hostility which Jesus provoked and the fact that the Easter experience resulted in a proclamation of *Jesus* as Lord.

Jesus believed his ministry of preaching and healing to be a
special 'time' (Mark 1: 15), in which the kingdom of God was not
merely at hand but even, in some sense, actually present (Matt. 12:
28 par.; Luke 17: 21). The situation of Jesus' disciples, who are able
to see and hear him, is uniquely privileged (Matt. 13: 16-17 par.; cf.
11: 4-6 par.). They are like wedding guests, for whom ascetical
practices are manifestly out of place (Mark 2: 19 par.), even though,
in an instruction to the disciples, Jesus seems to take such practices
for granted (Matt. 6: 16-18). If such judgements were expressed by
a religious leader today, we would probably assume that he was
either a madman or a charlatan. Whether they were any less extraordinary in the thought world of Jesus' day is a legitimate question,
but it concerns the apologist more directly than the historian.

'Christ', 'Suffering Servant', or 'prophet'?

It is difficult to say through which traditional titles Jesus' self-
understanding expressed itself. Only in the Fourth Gospel does
Jesus spontaneously affirm that he is the Christ (John 4: 25-6). In
the scene at Caesarea Philippi Jesus responds to Peter's confession,
'You are the Christ' (Mark 8: 29 par.), with a charge to the disciples
'to tell no one about him' (v. 30). In the trial before the Sanhedrin
Jesus does give an affirmative answer to the high priest's question,
'Are you the Christ, the Son of the Blessed?' (Mark 14: 61-2). However, we have already noted the historical problem of this episode,
and the literary motivation behind the high priest's question is quite
evident: Jesus' confession is contrasted with Peter's denial (vv. 66-
72). Moreover, it should be noted that Jesus' response in the other

two synoptic gospels is not unequivocal (Matt. 26: 64; Luke 22: 67). In the trial before Pilate, Jesus' non-committal answer ('You have said so') to Pilate's question, 'Are you the king of the Jews?' (Mark 15: 2 par.), suggests that an admission of messiahship may, in effect, have been extorted from him. Although he did not conceive his mission in terms of Jewish messianic expectations, he could not categorically deny Pilate's direct question without seeming to deny the divine origin of his mission.

If this is the case, then the hypothesis that Jesus became aware of his messiahship when he was baptized by John in the Jordan (Mark 1: 9-11 par.) has no firm basis. The interpretative vision (vv. 10-11) is not a description of Jesus' experience. Rather, it expresses the significance—for the evangelist or his tradition—of Jesus at the moment of his baptism. It has even been proposed that Jesus explicitly repudiated the messianic title. His rebuke to Peter at Caesarea Philippi, 'Get behind me, Satan!' (Mark 8: 33 par.) has been taken to be a direct response to Peter's confession of Jesus as the Christ (v. 29). But it is hard to understand how the earliest Christian creed could affirm, without apology or explanation, that 'Christ died' (1 Cor. 15: 3), if Jesus had explicitly rejected the use of this title.

All that can be said, therefore, is that Jesus is acclaimed as the Christ in a Christian sense only after his death. Although he aroused messianic expectations among the people and even among his own disciples, the contemporary understanding of the Messiah's role was incompatible with the death which he was to undergo in Jerusalem. This, undoubtedly, is why the evangelists have supplemented Peter's confession with a saying concerning the suffering, death, and resurrection of the Son of man (Mark 8: 31 par.). By itself, the Messiah title does not cast much light on Jesus' self-understanding. On the contrary, the title was reinterpreted in the light of Jesus' fate.

In the Lucan farewell discourse there is a citation of the fourth 'Servant Song': 'This scripture must be fulfilled in me, "And he was reckoned with transgressors"' (Luke 22: 37 = Isa. 53: 12). The Son of man saying in Mark 10: 45 par. contains an allusion to the same passage (Isa. 53: 10-12). The use of this passage to interpret Jesus' death seems the best explanation for the affirmation of the early creed that 'Christ died for our sins *in accordance with the scrip-*

tures' (1 Cor. 15: 3). Whether Jesus could have conceived of himself as the Servant of God depends, of course, on whether he reckoned with a violent death. It is generally believed that the passion prophecies which punctuate the latter half of Mark's account of Jesus' ministry (8: 31; 9: 31; 10: 33-4) look back on Good Friday and Easter Sunday. Not only is it difficult for the historian to imagine Jesus predicting his own resurrection, such precise predictions of the passion, with specific references to details from the passion narrative, namely the trial by the Sanhedrin, the handing over of Jesus to the Romans, the mocking, and the scourging, are not characteristic of authentic prophecy.

However, if Jesus' controversies with the scribes of the Pharisees are historical, we may suppose that Jesus undertook his final journey to Jerusalem, the centre of opposition to him (Mark 7: 1), with some foreboding of what awaited him there. Jesus' response to Herod's alleged attempt on his life may well contain an authentic saying: 'Behold, I cast out demons and perform cures today and tomorrow, and the third day I finish my course. Nevertheless, I must go on my way today and tomorrow and the day following, for it cannot be that a prophet should perish away from Jerusalem' (Luke 13: 32-3).

This saying suggests that Jesus could have identified himself with the role of the Suffering Servant; it also introduces the title 'prophet' (cf. Mark 6: 4 par.), which is of great significance for Jesus' self-understanding. In his response to the question of John the Baptist (Matt. 11: 2-6 par.) Jesus implicitly rejects the title 'he who is to come' (v. 3), referring John's disciples instead to his miracles and preaching (vv. 4-5). As the allusions to the book of Isaiah make clear (v. 5; cf. Isa. 29: 18-19; 35: 5-6; 61: 1), Jesus presents his 'deeds' (v. 2) as the fulfilment of the prophecies of the end-time.

In his earthly ministry Jesus is not Elijah, the fiery prophet of judgement (cf. Matt. 3: 11 par.; Mal. 3: 2; 4: 5; Ecclus. 48: 1); this role he assigns to John (Matt. 11: 14 par.). Jesus himself is anointed by God with the spirit 'to bring good tidings to the afflicted' (Isa. 61: 1; cf. Matt. 11: 5 par.; Luke 4: 18). Through his miracles and preaching the promised blessings of God's kingdom are made present. John was right in seeing in him an eschatological prophet, but his

particular mission is not to give warning of God's imminent judgement, as John had done, but rather to proclaim God's love and
forgiveness, to which the miracles bear witness. The fact that the
Servant Songs and the eschatological passages cited above are all
from the Book of Isaiah suggests that, in Jesus' mind, the 'servant'
and the 'eschatological prophet' may have been one and the same.

Jesus' miracles

To the rationalist spirit of the nineteenth-century quest, Jesus'
miracles were a provocation, and the most incredible explanations
were devised in order to distinguish the 'fact' recorded by the gospel
narrative from the 'opinion' which ascribed the event to supernatural
causes. The supernatural is not included among the causes with
which the historian is concerned. Nevertheless, he is not entitled to
reject *a priori* the occurrence of extraordinary events attested in his
sources simply because they are not part of his everyday experience.
One of Bultmann's students, Ernst Käsemann, has stated that if he
wished to remain a historian, he had no choice but to accept the
tradition that Jesus healed persons believed to be possessed by
demons. The problem of the miraculous is not limited to the pre-
scientific past. Even if we personally have never experienced anything which defies explanation, we are all aware of reliable reports
of such happenings.

Jesus' enemies acknowledged his miracles and accused him of
performing them with the assistance of 'the prince of demons'
(Matt. 12: 24 par.). This charge touched off a controversy which
culminates in Jesus' claim that his miracles are a sign that 'the
kingdom of God has come upon you' (v. 28). The *significance* of his
miracles, not their *occurrence*, is the issue at stake between Jesus
and his opponents. The fact that the occurrence of Jesus' miracles
was uncontested is a significant datum for the historian.

Of course, what was interpreted in Jesus' day in terms of supernatural intervention (whether divine or demonic) may suggest to
the modern reader explanations provided by scientific disciplines
unknown to the ancient world. But this is quite irrelevant to the
historical question under consideration. Jesus' claim that his miracles
were signs of the presence of the kingdom in his ministry gives us an

important insight into his self-understanding which alternative scientific explanations do not invalidate.

Jesus' parables

In the parables of Jesus we have a unique access to his historical personality. Of course, the parable, or *mashal*, was not invented by Jesus, but a study of Old Testament and rabbinic parables shows that his use of the form was distinctive. The parable, as an extended metaphor, uses the secular, everyday language of human experience, but it cracks the surface realism in order to give us a glimpse of something lying beyond it. As though through a screen or grid, we see something new and extraordinary which is not the direct object of affirmation at all.

The difference between the rabbinic parables and the parables of Jesus is not to be sought in the language used, even though Jesus often gives a new freshness to traditional imagery. The originality of Jesus' parables lies in the immediacy of the religious appeal to their hearers. The recital of a parable of Jesus constitutes 'the moment of truth' for whoever hears it, and his response to this hearing amounts to a self-judgement, for Jesus' parables—or at least many of them—proclaim an eschatological event, namely, the hidden presence of the kingdom in Jesus' ministry.

The parable of the sower (Mark 4: 3-9), for example, makes the point that God's royal rule will be manifested despite all obstacles. (The allegorical explanation in Mark 4: 13-20 par. has changed the point of the parable and is generally regarded as a later addition.) Despite the apparent failure symbolized by the grain devoured by birds, scorched by the sun, and choked by thorns, something radically new has happened with Jesus' coming, something intimately connected with the eschatological harvest in the kingdom of God. Recognition of this happening and acceptance of the consequences determine how the hearer will fare in the judgement.

The parable provokes a crisis by obliging the hearer to take a position with regard to the claim which it contains and the person making that claim, namely, Jesus himself. 'Everyone who acknowledges me before men, the Son of man also will acknowledge before the angels of God, but he who denies me before men will be denied before the angels of God' (Luke 12: 8-9). To the extraordinary claim contained in the parable corresponds the equally extraordinary claim implied in this saying, namely, that in the coming judgement Jesus himself ('Son of man' is a form of veiled self-designation) will have a role as advocate (cf. 1 John 2: 1), which he will exercise or not according to the stance taken toward him during his earthly ministry.

Jesus and apocalyptic

Such a saying makes clear that the context for Jesus' preaching was the apocalyptic thought world of his day, the discovery—so shocking to liberal theology—of Johannes Weiss (1892) and his star pupil, Albert Schweitzer. But Jesus' preference for metaphorical language when speaking of the kingdom of God suggests that we must modify the position of these pioneers in assessing the message of Jesus himself. Jesus' parables are told in the context of the impending crisis of divine judgement ('The kingdom of God is at hand; repent and believe in the gospel' (Mark 1: 15 par.)), and they summon the hearer to respond to the crisis of Jesus' coming. Nevertheless, the subject matter of the kingdom parables is never directly described.

As J. Jeremias has reminded us, on the basis of his study of the Aramaic background, the formula which introduces many of these parables is not to be translated 'The kingdom of heaven is like . . .' but rather 'This is the way things stand with the kingdom of heaven.' The indirect style of the story-teller is particularly understandable if, as the Targumic material suggests, 'the kingdom of God' is an alternative expression for God himself. Jesus' teaching is not an apocalyptic dogmatic. His parables are an imaginative redescription of reality based on his own profound experience of God.

Jesus' experience of God

This experience is expressed in the Aramaic word 'Abba', which occurs in the Marcan version of Jesus' prayer in Gethsemane (Mark 14: 36). The Greek equivalent occurs in the Lucan version of the Lord's Prayer (11: 2), in Jesus' cry of exaltation (Luke 10: 21 par.), and in one of the words on the cross (Luke 23: 46). Whatever may be said about the genuineness of these particular passages, they bear witness to Jesus' way of praying, which was continued within the early Christian community (cf. Rom. 8: 15; Gal. 4: 6).

J. Jeremias's study of 'Abba' has exaggerated the uniqueness of this way of addressing God, which is paralleled both in Palestinian (Ecclus. 51: 10) and Diaspora Judaism (Wisd. 14: 3). Nevertheless, Jesus' use of 'Abba' is a precious indication of his attitude towards God, which moderates an interpretation of his life and message exclusively in terms of contemporary apocalyptic. The title reflects a profound trust, which is also expressed in Jesus' response to an anxious question from his disciples (Mark 10: 26 par.): 'all things are possible with God' (v. 27). When Schweitzer represents Jesus' life as a progression from one erroneous apocalyptic conception to another, he is ignoring this crucial element. Jesus shared his contemporaries' expectation of the imminent end of the world (Mark 9: 1 par.; 13: 30 par.), while denying all knowledge of 'that day or that hour' (Mark 13: 32 par.); but he responded to external events with a deepened understanding of God's will for him, which he accepted with a trust based on love.

Jesus' imaginative redescription of reality can best be illustrated by the 'parables of mercy' (Luke 15: 1-32). The unrealistic behaviour of the protagonists (vv. 4, 6, 9, 20, 22-3) points to what is really at issue, though never mentioned in the parables themselves: the exuberant and unbounded love of God for sinners (vv. 7, 10). This great 'good news' gives to Jesus' ministry the quality of a wedding feast (Mark 2: 19 par.), just as John's call to penance was reflected in the fasting of his disciples (v. 18).

Jesus' table fellowship with 'tax gatherers and sinners'

Jesus gave visible expression to this understanding of his ministry in the practice of table fellowship. In so far as these common meals contrasted with John's asceticism, they earned Jesus the reputation of 'a glutton and a drunkard' (Matt. 11: 19 par.). In so far as they were shared with persons whose life-style put them beyond the pale of Judaism, they led to Jesus being dubbed 'a friend of tax collectors and sinners' (Matt. 11: 19 par; Luke 15: 2). In so far as they suggested that God's mercy was to be had for the asking (cf. Luke 18: 13-14), they expressed Jesus' authority to declare sins forgiven

(Mark 2: 5 par.), even before the sinner had given proof of his sincerity by bearing 'fruit that befits repentance' (Matt. 3: 8 par.). Such an initiative, whether by word or by deed, was considered a blasphemous infringement on God's exclusive rights (Mark 2: 7 par.).

The ethics of Jesus

The radicality of Jesus' ethical demands is part of his imaginative redescription of reality. The limitless forgiveness which a disciple of Jesus must offer a repentant brother (Matt. 18: 21-2 par.) is a consequence of the infinite mercy which he knows he has received from God (Matt. 18: 23-35). Just as Jesus appeals to the divine mercy in responding to the accusation that 'he receives sinners and eats with them' (Luke 15: 2), so he makes it the measure for the mercy which his disciples must show: 'Be merciful, even as your Father is merciful' (Luke 6: 36).

This requirement is best illustrated by Jesus' command to love one's enemies (Luke 6: 27 par.), perhaps the most characteristic element in his ethical teaching. Like the broader command (Mark 12: 31 par. = Lev. 19: 18), of which it is, so to speak, the test case (cf. Luke 10: 29), love of enemies is an imitation of the action of God, who 'is kind to the ungrateful and the selfish' (Luke 6: 35 par.). The impracticality of Jesus' ethics stems from the fact that it is not based on a commonly accepted view of the way things are in the world but rather on the imaginative redescription of reality which he invites his hearers to share, for example, in the parable of the good Samaritan (Luke 10: 30-5).

The characterization of Jesus' moral teaching as an 'interim ethic', which, though severe, need only be practised during the short period that precedes the arrival of God's imminent kingdom, misses the point altogether. Jesus' teaching *is* an ethic of the kingdom, but the kingdom has already become a reality—to be accepted through faith—in Jesus' own ministry. His preaching and miracles have ushered in the 'new covenant' (1 Cor. 11: 25; Luke 22: 20) prophesied by Jeremiah (31: 31): 'I will put my law within them, and I will write it upon their hearts, and I will be their God, and they shall be my people' (v. 33).

Jesus' radical demand for a religion of the heart (Mark 7: 20-3 par.) abrogates the external observance of the law as the way to God (cf. Matt. 5: 21-2, 27). The only appropriate response to the divine mercy is the total and unconditional surrender of the whole person. The trust expressed in the 'Abba' title prevents the disciple from looking forward to a reward in the calculating spirit of the elder son in the parable (Luke 15: 25-30). Although Jesus repeatedly holds out the promise of an eschatological reward (e.g. Matt. 6: 20 par.), he represents it not as earned wages but as a gift coming from God's unfathomable and undeserved generosity (cf. Matt. 20: 1-16, esp. v. 15). 'When you have done all that is commanded you, say "We are unworthy servants; we have only done what was our duty"' (Luke 17: 10).

Jesus and the Baptist

In discussing Jesus' self-understanding, we have had occasion to cite sayings in which he compares or contrasts himself with the Baptist. If the ambiguous phrase 'since then' (Luke 16: 16) may be interpreted, in the light of the Matthean parallel (Matt. 11: 12), as including John, rather than excluding him, then Jesus understands the Baptist and himself to be introducing a new period in which the scriptures ('the law and the prophets') find their fulfilment.

From the beginning, Jesus' career was closely intertwined with that of the Baptist, and the Lucan infancy narrative has carried this connection back to an encounter between the two cousins (cf. Luke 1: 36) while they both were still in their mothers' wombs (v. 41). Next to the crucifixion, the most indubitable fact in Jesus' ministry is his baptism by John in the Jordan (Mark 1: 9 par.). Although the tradition has made this event the occasion for Jesus to be proclaimed God's 'beloved son' (Mark 1: 11 par.), it was obviously an embarrassment for the evangelists. For all the gospels affirm Jesus' superiority to John, and the Baptist's prophecy that 'he who is mightier than I is coming' (Mark 1: 7 par.) was seen to be fulfilled in Jesus' appearance (Mark 1: 9 par.). To solve this difficulty, Matthew has interpolated a dialogue between Jesus and the Baptist, in which the latter protests: 'I need to be baptized by you, and do you come to me?' (Matt. 3: 14). The paradoxical baptism of the greater by the lesser is necessary 'to fulfil all righteousness' (v. 15).

Some scholars believe that the tradition is covering up a connection which would have been even more difficult to reconcile with Jesus' superiority than his baptism, that is, his membership in the group of the Baptist's disciples. The expression 'he who comes after me' (Matt. 3: 11 par.) can refer to discipleship (cf. Mark 8: 34), although the context suggests that the preposition should be taken in a temporal sense. If Jesus had been a follower of John, we would have an excellent explanation for his special interest in him. However, such a supposition is no more than a guess, and the significance of the Baptist for Jesus' self-understanding is clear in any case.

The gospels differ in the chronological relationship between the ministries of John and Jesus. The Fourth Gospel represents them as baptizing simultaneously (John 3: 22-3), suggesting, perhaps, that Jesus and his disciples originally constituted a rival sect which also practised baptism (cf. v. 26). (A later redactor has challenged the statement that Jesus baptized (John 4: 2)). Mark and Matthew make John's arrest the occasion for the beginning of Jesus' preaching (Mark 1: 14 par.). Luke has John arrested even before Jesus' baptism (Luke 3: 19-20), so that it is no longer clear by whom 'Jesus had been baptized' (v. 21).

The sequence in the synoptics may be the result of theological considerations: the 'inferior' is removed from the scene before the coming of the 'superior', or, at least, before he begins his ministry. But even if the two ministries are separated, a common fate is underlined by the use of the same verb: John is 'handed over' (Mark 1: 14 par.) just as the Son of man will be 'handed over' (Mark 9: 31 par.; 10: 33 par.). The verb in both cases is the same as the one that appears in the Greek translation (Septuagint) of Isa. 53: 12: 'he was handed over on account of our sins.'

There are sayings in the gospels which appear to reflect Jesus' meditation on the Baptist's fate. In Matt. 11: 16-18 par. he compares his contemporaries ('this generation') to spoiled children who persistently refuse their playmates' invitation, no matter what kind of game is proposed. The application of the parable is seen in the treatment of John and Jesus ('the Son of man'). Although their life-styles are markedly different, they experience a common fate of rejection. John's asceticism is taken as a sign of madness ('he has a demon'; cf. Mark 3: 21-2); Jesus' ordinary manner of living is met with a slurring reference to his practice of table fellowship ('Behold, a glutton and a drunkard, a friend of tax collectors and sinners!').

In a dialogue with the disciples which Mark has placed just after the transfiguration (Mark 9: 9: 'as they were coming down the mountain'), Jesus appears to allude to the fatal outcome of this rejection of both John and himself. Responding to a question of the disciples, Jesus reaffirms the traditional doctrine that Elijah must return 'first' (v. 11), 'before the great and terrible day of the Lord' (Mal. 4: 5), 'in order to restore all things' (Mark 9: 12; cf. Mal. 4: 6). But then, in a bold historicization of this teaching, he affirms, 'Elijah has come, and they did to him whatever they pleased, as it is written of him' (Mark 9: 13). As the Matthean parallel makes explicit, 'he was speaking to them of John the Baptist' (Matt. 17: 13).

Although suffering was not part of the traditional understanding of Elijah's return, it was the fate of the historical Elijah (1 Kgs. 19: 1-2, 10, 14), whom Jesus understands as foreshadowing the Baptist, who was imprisoned and executed (Mark 6: 17-29 par.). Between the two sayings about Elijah comes a reference to the Son of man: 'how is it written that he should suffer many things and be treated with contempt?' (Mark 9: 12). The implication is that the traditional teaching about Elijah's return does not contradict but rather confirms the necessity of Jesus' suffering.

Schweitzer's view that the failure of Jesus' Galilean ministry led him to believe that God had given him the commission 'to serve the members of the kingdom in the present, to give his life for them' (Mark 10: 45) is a plausible reconstruction. Without attempting to divide Jesus' ministry into precise phases, an undertaking for which our sources provide no basis, we can say that Jesus' appeal for conversion (Mark 1: 15 par.) presupposed the hope that it would be accepted. The ensuing disappointment may be reflected in Jesus' saying that 'for those outside [the circle of the disciples] everything is in parables' (Mark 4: 11 par.), i.e. everything is a riddle. In any case, it must have become apparent to him that he had not only antagonized the scribes but had also lost the support of the ordinary people. This realization could have led to the conviction that his ministry, like the ministry of the Baptist, must end tragically. His final journey to Jerusalem would then be neither an unwitting act of folly nor a deliberate provocation; it would be a prophetic gesture, a final appeal for conversion, which could only lead to death.

Jesus and the new covenant

However, Schweitzer failed to note the difference between the ministries of Jesus and the Baptist. Jesus distinguished his eschatological role from that of John (Matt. 11: 2-6 par.): The Baptist's task was to preach the imminence of the day of judgement and to summon his hearers to repentance before it was too late (Mark 1: 7-8 par.). Jesus continued John's ministry (Mark 1: 14-15), but his special task was to make present through his preaching and miracles God's merciful offer of forgiveness. If Jesus came to realize that he must die for the sake of his mission, he conceived his death not as the necessary catalyst for the final tribulation, as Schweitzer supposed, but as the seal of the new covenant (Luke 22: 20; 1 Cor. 11: 25).

According to the first three gospels and the apostle Paul, Jesus, on the night before he died, took bread, broke it, and said, 'This is my body'. Two of these texts add an explanation for this prophetic gesture: 'my body which is [given] for you' (1 Cor. 11: 24; Luke 22: 19). Although some critics believe that this interpretation belongs to the early church, an understanding of Jesus' death—symbolized by the broken bread—as being for others is in keeping with his understanding of his life, as expressed in word and deed.

Undoubtedly, Jesus' continuing attraction is to be explained in good part by his understanding of himself as a man for others. Yet his life is unintelligible apart from his acceptance of his mission from God, whose messenger he believed himself to be (cf. Isa. 52: 7). His table fellowship with outcasts, his healing of the sick, his liberation of those considered possessed by demons were all intended to set people free from their brokenness and alienation and to bring them into the presence of God's redeeming love.

Conclusion

No single method can bridge the chronological gap between Jesus and the canonical gospels, which are our sole sources for reconstructing his history. If the Jesus tradition is not the spontaneous creation of the Christian community, neither has it been transmitted by an official group within the church, who would have been entrusted with the verbatim memorization of Jesus' words and deeds. A study of the tendencies in the synoptic gospels and of oral tradition in primitive societies may cast some light on the history of the Jesus tradition prior to the first written gospel. However, the achievement of the later evangelists was to redact and expand a written source (Mark, in the case of Matthew and Luke; the Gospel of Signs, in the case of John). (See G. N. Stanton, *The Gospels and Jesus*, in this series, for a fuller discussion.) Mark's accomplishment in producing the first written gospel from largely oral sources was of quite a different character.

The literary model, best exemplified in Matthew and Luke, is even less useful in reconstructing the oral phase of the tradition. We cannot assume that the methods used by the evangelists in their *written* gospels were being used in the earlier period. For each oral recitation is a creative event in itself and therefore essentially different from the literary use made of a fixed written source. As far as modern folk-lore studies are concerned, it must be remembered that the transmission of oral tradition depends upon the sociological structure of the group. Unfortunately, our knowledge of the sociology of earliest Christianity is even more fragmentary than our knowledge of Jesus.

But if there is no simple formula for moving from the canonical gospels to the earliest level of community tradition or to Jesus himself, the situation for the historian is not quite so desperate as has sometimes been suggested. For if we leave all theological bias aside, historical probability suggests that the Jesus tradition originated in the impact made on Jesus' followers by his person, his teaching, and his actions. It is quite untrue to say that the historian is interested in who Jesus *was* but the Jesus tradition is only interested in who he *is*. Christians were quite capable of distinguishing between Jesus' earthly ministry and 'the days after the bridegroom has been taken away from them' (Mark 2: 19-20 par.), and the concerns of the latter period did not blot out all interest in the former.

There *is* a difference in interest between the modern historian and the early church which transmitted the Jesus tradition, but it is not along the lines of past *versus* present. The historian seeks to reconstruct an impartial account of Jesus' life, personality, and teaching which will seem plausible to his contemporaries, whatever their religious beliefs. The tradition, on the other hand, bears witness to a man whose life is judged to have been of unique religious significance. This significance is often brought out in the very manner in which the material is presented. Exposition and interpretation are not kept separate, as in modern historiography.

Whatever historical elements there may be in the traditions in the Fourth Gospel about the call of the disciples, the quality of the first followers' reactions to Jesus (John 1: 41, 45, 49) undoubtedly characterized the transmission of the Jesus tradition from its very beginning. There never was, in all probability, a detached, 'objective' reporting of Jesus' words and deeds. But the kerygmatic quality of the Jesus tradition does not render it useless for the historian. Indeed, to the extent that this quality reflects Jesus' impact on his contemporaries, it is of considerable historical importance.

As the earliest stories about Jesus were collected, the process of selection, which caused certain stories to be retold and not others, was governed by contemporary interests of the community. The same thing is true of the process by which, in the course of retelling, these stories were shaped and stylized, with certain features being given prominence and others being suppressed. Sometimes elements from different stories were conflated (cf. Mark 14: 3-9 par.). Naturally, from the standpoint of the historian, this process entails a regrettable loss. At times it has led to a refraction of the tradition such as to produce two or more quite different accounts of the same event. For example, the Johannine version of the call of the first disciples (John 1: 35-51) cannot be reconciled either with the account in Mark and Matthew of the call of the two pairs of brothers (Mark 1: 16-20 par.) or with the Lucan vocation story, where the spotlight is on Peter, whose call is connected with a miraculous catch of fish (Luke 5: 1-11; cf. John 21: 1-8).

The freedom of the tradition has created many problems for the historian which are simply insoluble. Nevertheless, this freedom had certain limits. The interest in what Jesus had said and done was never abandoned or suppressed because of contemporary concerns. Who Jesus *is* for the contemporary church has always been perceived to have a basis in who Jesus *was* during his lifetime. Moreover, the period during which the Jesus tradition was shaped—and partially garbled, from the historian's perspective—was relatively brief, from forty to sixty-five years, far less than the period separating the composition of other ancient lives from the figures whom they commemorate.

The history of the gospel tradition is such that there are many questions to which the historian will never be able to give an answer that is anything more than a guess. But there are other questions to which answers—more or less probable—*can* be given. This makes the work of reconstruction possible and, given the historical significance of Jesus, eminently worth the effort.

4

Lord and Spirit

The beginning of the Christian mission

1 Cor. 15: 3 is our earliest evidence for the fact that soon after Jesus' death his disciples began to preach him as the Christ, a title which comes from the translation into Greek of the Hebrew term 'Messiah'. Through this proclamation they bore witness to their belief that Jesus had been vindicated by God. The Messiah title, which was identical in meaning with the charge affixed to Jesus' cross ('the king of the Jews' (Mark 15: 26 par.)), was perceived to be rightfully his, not in the sense that he had been a political pretender, as the Romans may have feared (cf. Mark 15: 2 par.), but in the sense that he was Israel's redeemer king, who would save God's people from their sins (cf. Matt. 1: 21).

It has been plausibly argued that the early creed cited by Paul in 1 Cor. 15: 3 ff. is a Greek translation from Aramaic, the spoken language of most Jews living in Palestine. The book of Acts attests to the presence of Aramaic-speaking Jewish Christians in Jerusalem in its account of the dissension between the 'Hebrews' and the 'Hellenists' (Greek-speaking Jewish Christians) over the daily distribution to the widows (Acts 6: 1–6).

Acts makes Jerusalem the place where the Christian mission to Jews began. There Peter delivers a sermon to the 'men of Judaea and all who dwell in Jerusalem' (Acts 2: 14) on the Jewish Feast of Weeks (Shevuoth). This feast celebrated the first fruits of the wheat harvest (Exod. 34: 22) and received its name from the fact that it occurred seven weeks after passover (Lev. 23: 15–16; Deut. 16: 9–12), or on 'the fiftieth day'. This, in turn, explains the designation 'Pentecost' (Acts 2: 1), which is derived from the Greek numeral.

Although Acts makes clear that the first preaching was to Jews, the New Testament does not distinguish between the Jewish and Gentile missions when it attributes the origins of Christian preaching to a mandate of the risen Jesus (Acts 1: 8; Matt. 28: 19). According to Matthew, Jesus directs the Eleven to 'make disciples of *all nations*', and the Lucan Jesus, just before his ascension, declares to the apostles whom he had chosen (Acts 1: 2), 'You shall be my witnesses . . . to the end of the earth' (Acts 1: 8), i.e. Rome (cf. Acts 28: 16-31).

Since the historian is not competent to pass judgement on divine intervention in this world's affairs, he can neither affirm nor deny such a supernatural explanation. However, on the basis of the New Testament evidence itself, he must distinguish between the origins of the mission to the Jews and of the mission to Gentiles. The latter, which will occupy our attention in the next chapter, did not begin at the Pentecost following Jesus' death.

Whatever the factors which led to the Gentile mission, the decision to embark upon it took some time. The synoptic tradition records miracles performed by Jesus for the benefit of Gentiles (Matt. 8: 5-13 par.; Mark 7: 24-30 par.), which indicate a certain openness towards non-Jews on his part. But although such instances were undoubtedly perceived by the evangelists as anticipating the Gentile mission, there was no occasion in Jesus' historical ministry for him either to send his disciples to preach to Gentiles or to prohibit them from doing so, as he is represented as doing in Matt. 10: 5. Jesus took for granted that he and his disciples were sent to Israel (cf. Matt. 15: 24; 10: 6; Rom. 15: 8). The mission of the Seventy (Luke 10: 1), which recalls the table of the seventy nations (Gen. 10), may be an attempt to root a concern for the Gentiles in Jesus' ministry.

According to Acts, the decision to admit Gentiles to the church was made by Peter at Caesarea, after the Christian mission in Jerusalem and the surrounding areas was well under way. When he is called to account for his action by the 'circumcision party' in Jerusalem (Acts 11: 2), he defends himself not by an appeal to a command of the risen Christ but by narrating a vision which he had in Joppa (11: 4-10), the coincidental arrival of messengers from Caesarea (v. 11), and God's gift of the spirit to Cornelius and his household upon his arrival in that city (v. 15). This expansion of the Christian mission presupposes the mission 'to the people' (Acts 13: 31), i.e. the Jews, whose origin we shall examine in this chapter.

It has been proposed that the proclamation of Jesus as the Christ was simply the consequence of the disciples' reflection on their master's life and death. It can be shown with some plausibility that Jesus anticipated the violent end to which his activity would lead and accepted his death as willed by God. Could he not, then, have instructed his disciples in this point of view (cf. Luke 13: 33), so that, after his death, they proclaimed his vindication by God in terms of his resurrection? Some scholars claim that, according to contemporary Jewish expectations, God would reward the martyrdom of the eschatological prophet with resurrection (cf. Isa. 53: 10).

Such an historical reconstruction runs counter to the gospel accounts, which depict Jesus' death as a catastrophe for the disciples, which put an end to all their hopes (cf. Luke 24: 19-24) and fulfilled Jesus' prophecy, 'You will all fall away' (Mark 14: 27 par.).

Even if we assume that Jesus' own trust in God remained unshaken to the end, despite God's apparent rejection of him (Mark 15: 34 par.), there are no grounds for the view that at the time of Jesus' death the disciples were able to share this attitude. The traditions of their flight (Mark 14: 50 par.) and of Peter's denial (Mark 14: 66-72 par.) are strong evidence to the contrary, and Peter's tears over his disloyalty (Mark 14: 72 par.) need not indicate that he had come to terms with the prospect of his master's imminent execution.

Moreover, the two New Testament texts which are cited as evidence for Jewish belief in the resurrection of the martyred prophet are scarcely sufficient evidence. Herod's adoption of the popular opinion that Jesus is John the Baptist, brought back to life (Mark 6: 14, 16 par.), cannot be taken literally, since Jesus was already a grown man at the time of the Baptist's death. Rather, Jesus' ministry, as the continuation of the Baptist's, is perceived to be sustained by the same divine power which had animated him. The other text is no more convincing: the resurrection, after three and a half days, of two prophets martyred in Jerusalem (Rev. 11: 10-11) seems to be influenced by Christian belief. There simply is no evidence, contemporary with the New Testament, to suggest that the disciples were able, on the basis of Jewish beliefs, to interpret the crucifixion as calling for an act of divine vindication through Jesus' resurrection. It would, on the contrary, have been interpreted, in Jewish terms, as a sign of God's curse (cf. Gal. 3: 13 = Deut. 21: 23).

If the proclamation of Jesus as the Christ cannot be adequately explained as the result of theological reflection by disciples whose faith in him was confirmed, rather than destroyed, by the events of Good Friday, then the historian is obliged to enquire: what must have happened *after* Jesus' death to account for the disciples' conviction that, despite his shameful end, God had made him 'Lord and Christ' (Acts 2: 36)?

Once again, the New Testament writings are our only source in attempting this work of historical reconstruction, and there we find the Easter proclamation connected with a) the empty tomb story, and b) the appearance of Jesus after his death.

The empty tomb

Precise chronological indications in the gospels are quite rare; even the relation of Good Friday to the passover cannot be fixed with certainty (contrast Mark 14: 12 par. with John 18: 28). All the more striking, therefore, is the chronological indication which accompanies all four versions of the empty tomb story: 'on the first day of the week' (Mark 16: 2 par.). The possible historical significance of this phrase has often been overlooked, since it occurs in a story of an angelic apparition. In the Marcan form of the pericope the empty tomb serves principally as the place where Jesus' resurrection is proclaimed by a heavenly messenger, who gives it divine authority; the empty tomb itself is quite secondary.

The precise dating of heavenly visions is not unparalleled (cf. Ezek. 1: 1), and theological explanations have been given for the words 'on the first day of the week'. However, the phrase may also point to an occurrence which could have formed the historical nucleus behind the present kerygmatic form of the story: the women's journey to the tomb on the Sunday after Jesus' death.

The empty tomb has become an embarrassment to some modern

theologians, since it implies an understanding of the resurrection in terms of the resuscitation and/or transformation of a corpse, quite a different conception from that put forward today on the basis of contemporary philosophical anthropology. Some contemporary theologians, who reject the notion of the soul as separable from the body, view resurrection not as an event distinct from death but rather as death itself, seen from the side of eternity. Death is not simply the cessation of temporal existence but also the last free act of a spiritual being, *in* which he makes a final decision about himself and his life and *through* which he attains a definitive state of existence.

In terms of such an understanding, Jesus' empty tomb would not be a sign of his resurrection but simply an unexplained and perplexing phenomenon. This theological problem seems to be the reason why historical reconstructions have been offered for which there is not the slightest evidence. For example, it has been suggested that Jesus was buried in a pit for common criminals, and that the entire tradition of his burial in Joseph's tomb is sheer fabrication. Alternatively, it has been proposed that the women went to the wrong tomb, or that the body had been moved to a different tomb between the burial and their visit.

We need not enter into a debate over whether or not the empty tomb is a persuasive sign, in the twentieth century, of Jesus' resurrection almost two thousand years ago. Our concern is with the historical origin of the post-Easter mission, and our only question is whether the discovery of the empty tomb could have served as a catalyst for the Easter faith in an historical context in which the end of the world and the resurrection of the dead were expected imminently.

Even if the tradition is a problem for the theologian, it deserves to be taken seriously by the historian. The pre-Pauline *kerygma* and the pre-Marcan empty tomb story are both older than the books in which they appear, so that the relative dating of 1 Corinthians and Mark's gospel is quite irrelevant. Although the central role of the interpreting angel in the story would seem to be a theological development, the empty tomb itself has as much claim to consideration as the tradition of Jesus' appearances. There is no historical reason for regarding it as a secondary appendage, invented to emphasize the corporeality of the resurrection.

All the gospels indicate that the location of Jesus' tomb was well known. The Marcan burial story concludes with the words 'Mary Magdalene and Mary the mother of Joses saw *where he was laid*' (Mark 15: 47). The Fourth Gospel even describes Jesus' tomb as located in 'a garden in the place where he was crucified' (John 19: 41). It is highly unlikely that the two witnesses in Mark are an invention of the community, since the testimony of women had no legal force. Moreover, their mention was a painful reminder that none of Jesus' male disciples were present. Jesus' burial was arranged by an outsider, Joseph of Arimathea (Mark 15: 42-6 par.). Even Bultmann found no reason to question the basic historicity of the Marcan burial account, which, apart from Pilate's request for certification of Jesus' death (Mark 15: 44-5a), is sober and non-tendentious. (Vv. 44-45a could have been inserted to exclude an explanation of Jesus' 'resurrection' in terms of his merely apparent death.)

If the location of Jesus' tomb was known, then the tradition that it was found empty (Mark 16: 6: 'he is not here') cannot be lightly dismissed. For the contemporary Jewish understanding of resurrection was precisely a resurrection *of the body* (cf. Dan. 12: 2; John 5: 28-9; Matt. 27: 52-3). Consequently, the proclamation of Jesus' resurrection to Jews would have been quite impossible, if it had been known that his body was still in the tomb.

We find no trace of any Jewish polemic to the effect that the location of Jesus' tomb was unknown or that Jesus' body was still in it. On the contrary, Matthew reports that the chief priests and elders bribed the soldiers to circulate the story that Jesus' disciples had stolen his body while they were asleep (Matt. 28: 11-15). Particularly since the episode of the guard at the tomb (Matt. 27: 62-6) seems to have been inserted precisely in order to exclude the possibility of body-snatching, Matthew's concluding observation that 'this story has been spread among the Jews to this day' (Matt. 28: 15) must be taken seriously. The Jews did not deny that Jesus' tomb was empty; they had their own explanation for how this had come about (cf. John 20: 13, 15). The same can be said of modern Jewish historians.

The flight of the disciples

Mark's account of Jesus' arrest concludes with the embarrassing acknowledgement that all Jesus' disciples abandoned him and fled (Mark 14: 50). Since the women are instructed to convey to them the angel's message (Mark 16: 7 par.; cf. Matt. 28: 10; Luke 24: 9), the disciples are evidently supposed to have remained in hiding in Jerusalem (cf. John 20: 19). Nevertheless, it is in Galilee that an encounter with the risen Lord is to take place (Mark 14: 28; 16: 7). These two verses appear to have been placed in their present position by the evangelist and may even have been formulated by him. Nevertheless, they seem to reflect what would have been a natural reaction by the disciples to the catastrophic turn of events—a return to their home in Galilee. Under the circumstances produced by Jesus' arrest, it is unlikely that the regulations governing the passover and the sabbath would have prevented their immediate departure from the city.

In Mark's gospel the last episode involving one of Jesus' male disciples is Peter's denial (Mark 14: 66-72). They are absent from Jesus' crucifixion and burial and are not involved in the discovery of the empty tomb. (Luke 24: 12, 24 and John 20: 2-10 reflect a later stage of the tradition.) All this suggests that the hypothesis of their flight to Galilee may not, after all, be a legend of the critics. For if the disciples had actually been in Jerusalem when the empty tomb was discovered, it is difficult to find a motive for their journey back to Galilee.

Even though Luke has placed the story of Jesus' appearance to the two disciples at Emmaus (Luke 24: 13-32) on Easter Sunday, after the sabbath rest (Luke 23: 56), it may have had its original setting in a general flight of the disciples from Jerusalem soon after Jesus' arrest.

It is impossible to arrange in any plausible chronological sequence the resurrection appearances of Jesus to his male disciples in *both* Jerusalem (John 20: 19-23, 26-9; Luke 24: 34, 36-9) *and* Galilee (Matt. 28: 16-20; John 21: 1-23). The tradition that Jesus appeared to his male disciples in the holy city seems to be a secondary development, which culminates in Luke's localization of *all* the appearances in or near Jerusalem (contrast Luke 24: 6-7 with Mark 16: 7; cf. Acts 1: 4). The earliest gospel associates the male disciples with Jesus' appearance in Galilee and the women with the tomb just outside Jerusalem. In the later gospels the Lord appears also to Mary Magdalene (John 20: 16-18), together with 'the other Mary' (Matt. 28: 1, 9), and male disciples are connected with the empty tomb story (Luke 24: 12, 24; John 20: 2-10). These criss-crossing tendencies in the development of the tradition suggest that the discovery of the empty tomb and the appearances were originally unconnected: the women remained in Jerusalem, while the disciples fled to Galilee.

The earliest witness to the appearances (1 Cor. 15: 5 ff.) makes no reference to either Jerusalem or Galilee. Nevertheless, the traditions contained in 1 Cor. 15 and Mark 16 are not completely unrelated. Although the reference to Jesus' burial (1 Cor. 15: 4) does not mention the *empty* tomb, the affirmation that 'he was raised' would have been incompatible, in contemporary Jewish thinking, with the presence of Jesus' body in the tomb. Moreover, there may well be a connection between the chronological phrases included in the two resurrection traditions: 'on the third day' and 'on the first day of the week' (Mark 16: 2).

Since there were no witnesses to the resurrection itself, and since the appearances are assumed to have taken place at various times, some have attempted to connect 'on the third day' with the phrase which follows: 'according to the scriptures'. But although this could be an allusion to Hos. 6: 2 ('After two days he will revive us; on the third day he will raise us up'), this particular Old Testament text is never cited explicitly in the New Testament. (In Matt. 12: 40 Jonah's presence in the belly of the whale for 'three days and three nights' is secondarily linked to Jesus' presence in the tomb.) But if we count the Friday on which Jesus died, then 'the first day of the week', Easter Sunday, was indeed the third day, and the affirmation that Jesus' resurrection took place on that day could be an inference from the discovery of the empty tomb.

It is often said that, by itself, the discovery of the empty tomb is insufficient for the act of Easter faith, since there are other explanations for the absence of Jesus' body besides his resurrection. But

such a consideration has no place in evaluating the historical plausibility of gospel tradition. The gospels suggest that there was a
variety of catalysts for faith in Jesus' resurrection.

In the Emmaus story Jesus makes himself known to the two
disciples 'in the breaking of the bread' (Luke 24: 35). This suggests a
mysterious awareness of the Lord's presence during the fellowship
meals which he had instituted during his ministry and had ordered to
be continued, in the course of the farewell meal on the night before
he died (1 Cor. 11: 24, 25). Earlier in the same story the disciples
exclaim, 'Did not our hearts burn within us while he talked with us
on the road, *while he opened to us the scriptures*' (Luke 24: 32).
Here the scriptures seem to have mediated the conviction that Jesus
was alive and had sent his spirit to open the disciples' minds to the
inner meaning of 'Moses and all the prophets' (v. 27). The beloved
disciple comes to faith by seeing the grave cloths lying in the tomb
(John 20: 5, 8). The modern critic has no right to determine, on the
basis of his theological criteria, what may or may not have given rise
to the Easter faith.

The appearances of Jesus

Just as theological considerations have influenced the historical
evaluation of the empty tomb tradition, so too rationalistic scepticism has affected the evaluation of the other 'happening' after Jesus'
death which is associated with the beginnings of the Christian mission:
the 'appearances' of Jesus to his disciples. We must therefore keep in
mind that visionary experiences did not always have the association
with mental disturbance which they seem to have for us today. Jesus
himself is said to have seen 'Satan fall like lightning from heaven'
(Luke 10: 18), and Paul claims to have been taken up to 'the third
heaven' (2 Cor. 12: 2). In an age which took for granted the possibility of communication between heaven and earth, heavenly
visions and the hearing of 'things that cannot be told' (2 Cor. 12: 4)
were considered extraordinary, but not necessarily pathological.

The historian is not entitled to deny accounts of such phenomena
simply because they do not occur in his own experience, and to
dismiss them as hallucinations solves nothing. On the contrary, the

reality of such types of experience cannot be doubted, even though it is beyond the historian's competence to affirm or deny their divine origin.

Apart from Mark, with its paradoxical ending (Mark 16: 8), the gospels subordinate the empty tomb story to the appearance narratives. This may be due, in part, to the fact that the empty tomb was initially associated with female disciples, whose testimony had no legal force. Moreover, the empty tomb could be given other explanations besides the one proclaimed by the interpreting angel.

But despite the prominence given to these stories, they are of limited value for our enquiry into the origin of the Christian mission. For although they bear eloquent witness to the Easter faith, they do not help the historian in his efforts to discover the origin of this faith. The chronological and geographical indications in these narratives are so various and conflicting, and the influence of ecclesiastical concerns on their composition is so obvious that, quite apart from their extraordinary content, they cannot be taken as historical accounts.

The pre-Pauline credo

Consequently, the historian's interest is directed primarily to the pre-Pauline *kerygma* in 1 Cor. 15, where the affirmation of Christ's death, burial, and resurrection is followed by a recurring formula: 'he appeared' (Greek *ōphthē*), plus a list of persons to whom 'he appeared'. If we leave out of consideration for the moment the appearance to Paul himself (v. 8), these persons include two individuals ('Cephas', i.e. Peter, and 'James') and three groups ('the Twelve', 'more than five hundred brethren', and 'all the apostles'). In this list Cephas is associated with the Twelve, and James is associated with 'all the apostles'.

There are a number of questions of importance for our enquiry which arise out of these verses: a) the connection of the *ōphthē* formula with the preceding confession of Christ's death and resurrection; b) the connection of the appearance to Cephas with the ones which follow; c) the original function of the *ōphthē* formula, particularly if 1 Cor. 15: 5-7 arose independently of the confession which precedes; d) the significance of *ōphthē*, as indicated by its use in the Greek Old Testament.

Paul's reason for citing this list is quite clear: as witnesses to Christ's appearances after his death, the persons mentioned can reassure the Corinthians concerning the reality of Jesus' resurrection and of the resurrection of the dead, with which, in Paul's view, the former is indissolubly linked (1 Cor. 15: 13, 16). The point of his parenthetical observation that 'most [of the more than five hundred brethren] are still alive' (v. 6) is to suggest to the Corinthians that this testimony is still available to resolve any doubts they may have. Moreover, by including in the list of appearances his own experience of Christ before Damascus (Gal. 1: 15-16), Paul associates himself with the other persons in the list.

In Paul's use of the early creed, Christ's resurrection (and the resurrection of the dead) is clearly an inference from the appearances. However, another early credal affirmation, also cited by Paul, that 'Jesus died and rose again' (1 Thess. 4: 14; cf. Rom. 6: 3-4), makes no mention of appearances. This suggests that the creed in 1 Cor. 15: 3-4 may have circulated independently of the list which follows. Indeed, Paul himself may have joined together the creed and the list of appearances precisely in order to meet the Corinthians' denial of the resurrection (1 Cor. 15: 12).

The appearance to Peter

It is generally held that the verb *ōphthē* ('he appeared') could not have circulated without the name of at least one person to whom Christ had appeared. Attention has focused on the appearance to Cephas (Peter), not only because he is the first name on the list, but also because an appearance to 'Simon' alone has been inserted, somewhat awkwardly, in the Emmaus story (Luke 24: 34), before the two disciples have an opportunity to tell the assembly of the Lord's appearance to them (v. 35). This emphasis on the 'primacy' of the appearance to Peter suggests that the other occurrences of the *ōphthē* formula in 1 Cor. 15 have been modelled on the first appearance in the list, which would then have grown by accretion. The fact that Paul's claim, 'he appeared also to me' (v. 8), is clearly an addition to what he has 'received' (v. 3) gives some substance to this hypothesis.

In fact, some have gone so far as to claim that the appearance to Peter was the *only* such experience apart from Paul's, and that his post-Easter name ('rock') expresses his 'church building' function (cf. Matt. 16: 18) of strengthening his 'brethren' (Luke 22: 32), that is, the other members of the Twelve, by communicating to them his Easter faith. While such a suggestion must remain quite hypothetical, it cautions us against making the opposite assumption, that the number of appearances must correspond either to the number of names in the list or to the fourfold occurrence of *ōphthē*.

Furthermore, the repetition of the verb does not entitle us to suppose that the personal experiences summarized in this list (however many there may have been) were all of the same type. Indeed, the very notion of 'appearances' is an objectivizing paraphrase easily open to misunderstanding. Its legitimate function is to point to a phenomenon where the demand for conceptual precision is out of place.

Considering the importance of the appearance to Peter, it is curious that he is not the central figure in any of the gospel apparition stories. This silence has been explained as a negative reaction to the 'primacy' of the appearance to Peter in the earlier tradition. In the Pseudo-Clementine literature, Peter is the defender of Jewish Christianity which observed the law, in opposition to Paul. (These 'Clementine' writings circulated in the early church under the name of Clement of Rome, who, in turn, was sometimes identified with the 'Clement' mentioned by Paul in Phil. 4: 3.) It would not be surprising, therefore, if the Gentile Christianity to which we owe the final form of the last three gospels (the original text of Mark contains no appearance stories) declined to preserve in narrative form the tradition of Jesus' first appearance to him.

However, two episodes now situated in the narrative of Jesus' ministry have been plausibly interpreted as resurrection appearances to Peter. The miraculous catch of fish (Luke 5: 1-11), where Jesus and Peter are the main characters, resembles the resurrection story in John 21: 1-8 and may have been transferred back to Jesus' earthly ministry. Jesus' words to Peter at Caesarea Philippi (Matt. 16: 17-19), which Matthew has inserted into the Marcan episode of Peter's confession (Mark 8: 27-33), may also have come from an original Easter setting. Not only is the reference to building a church (v. 18) difficult on the lips of the earthly Jesus; the phrase 'flesh and blood has not revealed this to you' (v. 17) resembles Gal. 1: 15-16, where Paul is speaking of his experience of the risen Lord.

'Seeing', 'seeing that', and 'revealing'

We cannot expect the verb *ōphthē* to disclose the character of the experience to which it points. Although the first appearance was to Peter, the use of this particular verb need not go back to him. Rather, *ōphthē* appears to be, like the verb which precedes it ('he was raised'), a community formulation.

In the gospel appearance stories, which all have to do with persons who knew Jesus during his earthly life, there is the recurring theme of recognition: Mary Magdalene exclaims, 'Rabboni!' (John 20: 16); Thomas, 'My Lord and my God!' (John 20: 29); the Beloved Disciple, 'It is the Lord!' (John 21: 7); the Emmaus disciples 'recognized him' (Luke 24: 31). This theme of recognition (*anagnōrisis*) is a familiar one in Greek literature, beginning with Homer; Odysseus is recognized, upon his return to Ithaca, by the scar from a wound inflicted on him years before by a wild boar (*Od.* xix 392-4).

However, the same verb *ōphthē* is used by Paul of his own experience, and it is generally agreed that Paul did not know Jesus during his earthly ministry. Consequently, 'seeing', in the sense of recognizing a former acquaintance, cannot be associated with every use of *ōphthē*. When Paul refers to his Damascus experience in Galatians, he uses different language: 'when he who had set me apart before I was born, and had called me through his grace [i.e. God], was pleased to *reveal his Son to me*' (1: 15-16). Here the experience is expressed not in terms of 'seeing' a person but in terms of a revelation by God concerning who that person is, i.e. God's Son. This formulation is especially important, since, unlike *ōphthē*, it comes from the person who actually had the experience. In fact, if we grant the common view that 1-2 Peter and the letter of James are pseudonymous, then Paul is the only person mentioned in the list in 1 Cor.

15: 5-8 whose writings have come down to us; his reference to his own experience therefore has unique significance.

Indeed, 'seeing', whether in Greek or English, is an ambiguous notion. It can be used with an object of either sensory or mental perception. We say both 'I see you' and 'I see what you mean'. The use of *ōphthē* for an experience of Peter, who had known the earthly Jesus, and of Paul, who had not, points to what was common to the two experiences—an insight into who Jesus was: the 'Christ' (1 Cor. 15: 3); the 'Son' of God (Gal. 1: 16). Although we cannot express in conceptual terms the nature of the experiences, we know that in each case they had a personal character: they mediated a new knowledge of Jesus, which was not available simply through reflection on his life and death.

Moreover, the source of this knowledge, in both experiences, is believed to be God himself. This is explicit in Paul, in his use of the verb 'to reveal' (Gal. 1: 16); it may also be present in the pre-Pauline *kerygma*, where *ōphthē* has been taken to be a 'theological passive': that is, God, whose name is left unmentioned out of respect, *caused* Christ to appear. In one of the Lucan speeches in Acts this understanding is made explicit: 'God raised [Jesus] on the third day and *made him manifest*, not to all the people but to us who were chosen by God as witnesses' (Acts 10: 40-1). Even in the case of those who had followed Jesus during his earthly ministry, 'seeing' him after his death was understood to be not a natural human act of sense perception, but an act of divine revelation (cf. Matt. 16: 17).

In the list in 1 Cor. 15: 5-8 all those mentioned, apart from the 'more than five hundred brethren', are persons or groups who held positions of authority in the early church: Peter, the Twelve, James, the apostles, Paul. It has therefore been suggested that the original function of the *ōphthē* formula was not to legitimate the preaching of Christ's resurrection, the use which Paul has made of it in addressing the Corinthians, but rather to legitimate the preacher—to suggest the divine origin of the mandate exercised by important church figures.

Paul's own use of the formula in 1 Cor. 15: 8 implicitly associates him with the group of 'the apostles' mentioned in the previous verse, thus countering the implication of '*all* the apostles' that Paul himself is not included. Moreover, in the other passage where Paul speaks of 'seeing' Jesus after his death, the context again suggests his concern that he be recognized as having the same status as the other apostles: 'Am I not an apostle? Have I not seen Jesus our Lord?' (1 Cor. 9: 1).

Both the Pauline use of the *ōphthē* formula to legitimate the preaching of the resurrection, and its suggested pre-Pauline use to legitimate the preacher, presuppose the existence of the Christian mission. Neither use, therefore, can be the original one. Rather, both presuppose the function of the formula which we have been considering—to point to the revelatory experience of who Jesus is, which led those who had the experience to proclaim him after his death as 'Christ' and 'Son of God'.

The Old Testament and intertestamental literature as background

Particularly if the appearances (1 Cor. 15: 5-7) circulated independently of the preceding confession (vv. 3-4), the proclamation of Christ's resurrection cannot have been a simple inference from the appearances. In itself, *ōphthē* does not imply resurrection. Elijah and Moses 'appeared' to the three disciples on the Mount of the Transfiguration (Mark 9: 4 par.). Although there was a popular tradition of the 'assumption' of Moses (cf. Jude 9), who had died and was buried (Deut. 34: 6), Elijah was believed to have been taken up to heaven while still alive (2 Kgs. 2: 11).

In the earlier writings of the Greek Old Testament, *ōphthē* is used of the appearances both of angels (e.g. Exod. 3: 2; Judg. 6: 12; 13: 3) and of God himself (e.g. Gen. 12: 7; 17: 1; 26: 2; Exod. 6: 3). In such instances there is evidently no connection with resurrection from the dead. (This Septuagintal usage is continued in the New Testament: God's appearance to Abraham [Acts 7: 2]; angelic appearances in Luke-Acts [Luke 1: 11; 22: 43; Acts 7: 30, 35].)

In the Old Testament such appearances are usually connected with a divine communication. The verb signifies God's revealing presence at crucial points in Israel's history. The use of *ōphthē* is therefore associated with divine revelation. But in a Jewish context Christ's appearances (1 Cor. 15: 5-8) can be a sign of his resurrection (1 Cor. 15: 4) only if joined to the affirmation of his death (1 Cor. 15: 3) and the complementary sign of the empty tomb (Mark 16: 6; cf. 1 Cor 15: 4). Only then is an interpretation of Jesus' appearance as the appearance of an angel (Acts 23: 9) or a ghostly apparition (Luke 24: 37; cf. Mark 6: 49) effectively excluded.

Belief in the resurrection of the dead is a rather late development in Judaism. It is clearly expressed in only one book of the Hebrew Bible, Daniel, written in the early second century BCE. Although attributed to one of the Jewish exiles in Babylon, during the reign of Nebuchadnezzar (605-562 BCE), the book of Daniel was actually written during the persecution of the Maccabean patriots by Antiochus Epiphanes (175-164 BCE). The writer declares that the campaign of Antiochus introduces the great tribulation which precedes the end of the world, when 'many of those who sleep in the dust of the earth shall awake, some to everlasting life, and some to shame and everlasting contempt' (Dan. 12: 2; cf. John 5: 28-9).

This belief, which may derive from the ancient Iranian religion, is not associated in Judaism with the concern for personal immortality which so dominated Egyptian thinking, for example. The resurrection of the dead was only the prelude to God's judgement, and its necessity arose out of the realization that the reward of the righteous and the punishment of the wicked were not always carried out in this life. Belief in the resurrection is therefore a consequence, in Jewish thinking, of belief in God's justice and, in particular, of God's vindication of his elect, who, as in the case of the Maccabean martyrs, have suffered persecution and death out of fidelity to God's law.

In the period just preceding the composition of the New Testament there was a great development in Jewish apocalyptic. Not only was the resurrection faith of Dan. 12: 2 further elaborated, but there was also much speculation concerning the interim state between death and resurrection. In the Wisdom of Solomon, written by a Hellenistic Jew some time during the first century BCE, we find the doctrine of the immortality of the soul: 'The souls of the righteous are in the hand of God, and no torment will ever touch them. In the eyes of the foolish they seemed to have died, and their departure was thought to be an affliction, and their going from us to be their destruction; but they are at peace. For though in the sight of men they were punished, their hope is full of immortality' (Wisd. 3: 1-4).

But although the author affirms the immediate union of the blessed with God after death, he does not adopt the Platonic view of the soul as sent into exile in the body and then liberated from the body at death. Jewish thinking remained concerned with the fate of the integral human being, and not of some privileged 'part' of the person. The resurrection of the body is the resurrection of the whole person, who does not *have* a body but *is* a body, a living being of 'flesh and blood'. The identity of the body guarantees the identity of the person. The *same* body must rise which was buried; only afterwards is there a gradual transformation into heavenly glory.

Jewish expectation of a resurrection of the dead at the end of the world facilitated the belief that God could raise a person to life in this world. Referring to the raising of the dead by Elijah (1 Kgs. 17: 17-24) and Elisha (2 Kgs. 4: 32-7), one rabbi affirmed, 'All that the Holy One (praised be he) will perform for his world in the age to come, he has already partially carried out and anticipated through the co-operation of his just prophets.' The New Testament contains stories of the resurrection of Jairus' daughter (Mark 5: 21-4, 35-43 par.), of the son of the widow of Nain (Luke 7: 11-17), and of Lazarus (John 11: 1-44).

The resurrection of Jesus and the historian

The affirmation that 'Christ was raised' (1 Cor. 15: 3-4) has its conceptual background in Jewish belief. Nevertheless, Jesus' resurrection differs significantly from both understandings of resurrection summarized above. On the one hand, it is clearly not the restoration of a dead person to continued temporal existence; on the other hand, it is not part of a collective resurrection immediately preceding God's final judgement. Rather, Jesus is declared to have been raised by God (theological passive) while 'this present age' continues to run its course. Although there were popular traditions about the 'assumption' of Moses, the resurrection *of a contemporary person* to life with God is without parallel in Jewish sources.

As an act of God, the resurrection of Jesus does not fall within the competence of the historian. It is accessible to him only in so far as it finds expression in faith affirmations, such as the one in 1 Cor.

15. But in our investigation of the origins of the Christian mission, the notion of resurrection has a crucial place. It makes clear that the revelatory event indicated by *ōphthē* mediated an insight into who Jesus *is*, not simply who he *was* during his earthly ministry. Consequently, an exclusively functional interpretation of Jesus' resurrection as the continuation, through the Christian mission, of Jesus' 'cause' is an inadmissible modernization of the pre-Pauline *kerygma*. 'Christ was raised' is not reducible to the platitude that he 'lives on' in the preaching of the community. The first Christian missionaries did not take up their activity simply out of a new awareness of the significance of their master and his teaching. They attributed the mission to God's intervention, which both vindicated Jesus and commissioned certain of his followers to proclaim him, not as a dead hero but as the living Lord.

The gift of the spirit

The Pentecost following Jesus' death not only marks the beginning of the Christian mission 'to the people' (Acts 13: 31); it was also the occasion of an event which was interpreted as the gift of the spirit (Acts 2: 4). The external manifestation of this gift is seen in the phenomenon that 'the company' (Acts 1: 15) 'speaks in other tongues' (Acts 2: 4). That is to say, Peter and those with him *speak* in Galilean dialect, but 'devout men' (v. 5), the Jewish pilgrims who have come 'from every nation under heaven' (v. 5) to Jerusalem (cf. John 12: 20), in order to observe the Feast of Weeks, *hear* them in their own several languages: 'Are not all these who are speaking Galileans? And how is it that we hear, each of us in his own native language? (Acts 2: 7-8).

Luke's concern in this narrative seems to be the miraculous reversal of the story of the tower of Babel (Gen. 11: 1-9), and there are indications that the phenomenon which actually attracted the pilgrims' attention has been altered to correspond with this theological purpose. For the language of the Galilean Christians was not intelligible to everyone. 'Others' present responded with the jibe, 'They are filled with new wine' (Acts 2: 13), and Peter feels obliged to answer this charge at the beginning of his speech: 'These men are not drunk, as you suppose, since it is only the third hour of the day' (v. 15).

This suggests that the external sign of the spirit's presence was actually glossolalia, a phenomenon referred to in Paul's list of 'charisms' (i.e. spiritual gifts) as 'various kinds of tongues' (1 Cor. 12: 10). He makes this particular gift the subject of an extended instruction to the Corinthian community (1 Cor. 14). Luke himself refers to this phenomenon, once in connection with the laying on of hands in Ephesus (Acts 19: 6), and once in connection with God's direct intervention in favour of Cornelius and his household (Acts 10: 46).

Glossolalia consisted in uttering, in an ecstatic state, certain unintelligible sounds or incoherent words, which could only be understood by someone with the corresponding charism of 'interpretation' (1 Cor. 12: 10; 14: 5, 13, 27). Unlike prophecy, whose purpose was to offer 'upbuilding and encouragement and consolation' (1 Cor. 14: 3), glossolalia merely attested the presence of the spirit in the community.

It has been suggested that Christ's 'appearance' to 'more than five hundred brethren' (1 Cor. 15: 6), about which we are given no further information, may, in fact, be identical with the gift of the spirit at Pentecost. The use of the term 'brethren' suggests that those involved were already Christians, and that the experience in question did not involve a new insight into Jesus' identity, as in the case of Peter (1 Cor. 15: 5) and Paul (Gal. 1: 16). The modern historian has difficulty imagining Christ's appearance to a group of persons, and the literary character of the group appearances in the gospels prevent us from using them as an argument for a literalistic interpretation of *ōphthē* in 1 Cor. 15: 6. As we have seen, *ōphthē* is a formula, and its repetition in 1 Cor. 15: 5-8 does not entitle us to assume that all the experiences referred to in this list were of the same type. We have examples of a literary use of the verb in connection with celestial appearances to a group both in the Old Testament ('the glory of the Lord appeared to all the people' (Lev. 9: 23)) and in the New Testament ('Elijah with Moses appeared to [Peter and James and John]' (Mark 9: 4; cf. v. 2)).

On the other hand, Paul clearly considers the 'more than five hundred brethren' to be witnesses to Christ's resurrection. This is consistent with the interpretation which we are proposing. For the gift of the spirit, as manifested in glossolalia, was considered proof of Jesus' exaltation, which gave him authority (cf. Matt. 28: 18), including the authority to impart 'in the last days' God's gift of the spirit (Acts 2: 17-21 = Joel 2: 28-32).

In ancient Israel ecstatic behaviour was associated with the coming of the spirit. Samuel tells Saul, 'The spirit of the Lord will come mightily upon you, and you shall prophesy with [a band of prophets] and *be turned into another man*' (1 Sam. 10: 6; cf. v. 5); when the time comes, Saul's behaviour prompts the question, 'What has come over the son of Kish?' (v. 11).

In the New Testament period, when the voice of the prophets had been stilled at least since Malachi (about 460-50 BCE), the gift of the spirit was associated with 'the last days' (Acts 2: 17), when communication between heaven and earth would be fully restored. The same kind of thinking which interpreted the appearance of Jesus after his death in terms of the resurrection of the dead, which precedes God's final judgement, also interpreted the appearance of glossolalia within the first Christian community as the sign of the presence of God's eschatological spirit.

In Eph. 4: 8 we find cited, in a form close to the Septuagint translation, the following psalm verse: 'When he ascended on high, he led a host of captives, and *he gave gifts to men*' (Ps. 68: 18). Although the interpretation of this verse is notoriously difficult, the author of the epistle appears to connect Jesus' exaltation with the bestowal upon the community of divine gifts or charisms. The same conception seems to be reflected in Peter's words at Pentecost: 'Being therefore exalted at the right hand of God, and having received from the Father the promise of the holy spirit, he has poured out this which you see and hear' (Acts 2: 33).

Conclusion

The connection between 1 Cor. 15: 6 and the Pentecost experience is only a hypothesis. The number of the company of Christian disciples, as reported by Luke ('about a hundred and twenty' (Acts

1: 15)), does not correspond to the 'more than five hundred brethren' mentioned by Paul. On the other hand, it is worth noting that the verb used to express the 'appearance' of 'tongues as of fire' (Acts 2: 3) is the same one used to express the 'appearance' of Christ in 1 Cor. 15: 6.

A clear distinction between the risen Lord and the spirit in which he was raised from the dead and which he in turn bestows on believers is a product of later theological reflection. Paul affirms, 'The Lord *is* the spirit' (2 Cor. 3: 17); through his resurrection, Christ, as the second Adam, *'became* a life-giving spirit' (1 Cor. 15: 45). This close association, not to say identification, of 'Son of God' and 'holy spirit' is expressed in the ancient hymn cited by Paul at the beginning of his Letter to the Romans: 'designated Son of God in power according to the spirit of holiness by his resurrection from the dead' (Rom. 1: 4).

The joining together of the Easter and Pentecost experiences is given dramatic expression in John 20: 19-23, where an appearance of the risen Lord (v. 19) is combined with his gift of the spirit to the disciples (v. 22). The spirit experienced by the Christians in the ecstasy of glossolalia was believed to be the spirit *of Christ*, and its bestowal pointed to Christ's exaltation, even as Jesus' appearance after his death and the sign of the empty tomb pointed to Christ's resurrection.

The origin of the Christian mission to Israel lies both in the memory of Jesus' life and death and in ecstatic experiences which were interpreted both christologically and eschatologically. The proclamation of Jesus as the Christ cannot be explained simply as the result of the disciples' reflection on the fate of their dead master. On the other hand, the Easter and Pentecost experiences were not given a value in themselves; they were both interpreted with reference *to Jesus* and resulted in a proclamation *of him* as Lord and Christ.

5

'Neither Jew nor Greek'

Christian self-definition and the New Testament

Events in history often have consequences quite unforeseen by the human actors and certainly unintended by them. From innumerable sequences of cause and effect, the historian selects those which are historically significant, fitting into a pattern of rational explanation and interpretation. One of the principal historical consequences of the writings which we today call 'the New Testament' was the emerging consciousness of those who read and used them that they belonged to a movement which was distinct both from Judaism and from the multiplicity of other cults which existed in the Graeco-Roman world.

In the latest writing contained in the New Testament, we see that the letters of Paul had already come to be regarded as 'scripture' (2 Pet. 3: 16; cf. Rom. 16: 26), on a par with the Old Testament books, which were the only 'scripture' which Paul himself had known. The formation of the New Testament canon in the second and third centuries would bring this process to its conclusion.

At the time that most of the New Testament books were being composed, such a self-understanding did not yet exist. The term 'Christian'—an expression of the movement's arrival at a certain stage of self-definition—only occurs three times, in two out of the twenty-seven books of the New Testament. It is important for the historian to consider not only those things in the New Testament which point ahead to the emergence of Christianity and its understanding of itself as a 'third race', but also to reconstruct the position which the New Testament authors and their communities occupied in relation to the Jewish matrix out of which they arose, as well as in relation to each other. In this way, we may hope to appreciate the significance of these writings for the historical development, without reading the self-understanding which they produced back into the historical situation in which the writings were composed.

Jewish self-understanding and the Jewish war

The self-understanding of Judaism underwent an important development during the period in which the New Testament books were being written. It is significant that the term 'Judaism' occurs only twice in the New Testament, in two successive verses of a Pauline epistle (Gal. 1: 13-14), both times referring to the apostle's own antecedents. In terms both of their self-understanding and the way in which they were viewed by others, the Jews were a 'people', which, like the other peoples within the Roman Empire, venerated their own deity. Although they referred to non-Jews as 'the Gentiles' (i.e. 'the nations') the Jews were well aware that they too constituted a 'nation' (cf. John 11: 50).

After the Jewish War, when the 'holy city' (Matt. 4: 5), Jerusalem, lay in ruins, and the 'holy place' (Matt. 24: 15), the temple, had been burned to the ground, it was the religious leaders, specifically those Pharisees who had not been involved in the uprising against Rome, who maintained a sense of national and religious identity. In part, the development of Christian self-consciousness was in reaction to the development of a new Jewish self-consciousness following the catastrophe of the year 70.

During the period between Jesus' crucifixion (*c.* 30) and the outbreak of the Jewish War (66), the pluralism of Jewish groups permitted Jewish Christians, or better, Christian Jews, to exist as one sect among many. Acts uses the expression 'the sect [*hairesis*] of the Nazarenes' (24: 5), as well as 'the sect of the Sadducees' (5: 17) and 'the sect of the Pharisees' (15: 5), and Paul is represented as exploiting to his own advantage the hostility between the two latter groups (23: 6-9).

The Pharisees, whose unification of Judaism after 70 ultimately led to the exclusion of 'the Nazarenes', appear not to have persecuted them during the earlier period. Indeed, they seem to have included 'some believers' among their number (Acts 15: 5; cf. 21: 20). A renowned Pharisee, Rabban Gamaliel the Elder, advises the Sanhedrin to take no action against Peter and the apostles (Acts 5: 34-9).

According to Acts 4: 1-3, it is the Sadducees who arrest Peter and John, and Herod Agrippa I, whose persecution of the community is narrated in Acts 12: 1-5, was an ally of the Sadducees. James, the brother of Jesus, was executed by the high-priest Annas (Josephus, *Ant.* xx. 200)—the son of the Annas mentioned in the New Testament (Luke 3: 2; John 18: 13, 24; Acts 4: 6). The indignation which this action produced among non-Christian Jews shows that there was no united Jewish opposition against the Nazarenes in the year 62.

Moreover, the persecution of one Jewish sect by another was no rarity. The Jewish priests who withdrew from the temple worship in Jerusalem in order to form a community at Qumran, on the shore of the Dead Sea, recalled how their leader, the Teacher of Righteousness, was 'pursued to the house of his exile' by 'the wicked priest' (1 QpHab 11: 4-6).

Conversely, polemical expressions directed by New Testament writers against 'the Jews' should not be taken as evidence that these writers no longer considered themselves or their communities to be Jewish. Paul tells the Thessalonians that they have suffered the same things from their countrymen as the churches of Judaea did 'from the Jews, who killed both the Lord Jesus and the prophets, and drove us out' (1 Thess. 2: 14-15). However, in another context Paul refers to himself as 'a Hebrew born of Hebrews' (Phil. 3: 5), and in defending his position against rival missionaries, he boasts, 'Are they Hebrews? So am I. Are they Israelites? So am I' (2 Cor. 11: 22). Attacks on 'the Jews' may bear testimony to a growing sense of alienation on the part of New Testament writers and their communities, but they do not prove a loss of Jewish identity or the presence of a new 'Christian' identity.

Nor can we assume that the New Testament writers and those whom they addressed all formed a united front. To be sure, there is only one instance in the New Testament where one writer refers explicitly to another (2 Pet. 3: 15), with a significant comment on Paul's writings: 'there are some things in them hard to understand' (v. 16). However, the spectrum of religious belief and practice reflected in the New Testament is every bit as broad as that which exists among Christians today, and relations would scarcely have been uniformly cordial. Moreover, in most books of the New Testament we find explicit criticism of other Christians, whose teaching or conduct is regarded as a threat to the community being addressed.

This complex situation may be represented diagrammatically, with the broken lines indicating divisions within the groupings.

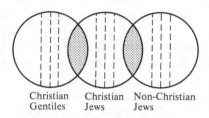

Christian Gentiles   Christian Jews   Non-Christian Jews

As the diagram indicates, the ethnic differential (Gentiles-Jews) was at least as important for the historical development as the religious differential (Christian-non-Christian).

The proclamation of Jesus as the Christ seems at first to have been a provocation only to the Sadducees, who, through their collaboration with the Romans, bore a special responsibility for Jesus' death, and therefore saw in the apostles' preaching an intent 'to bring this man's blood upon us' (Acts 5: 28). The book of Acts represents the Jerusalem community as participating in the daily temple cult, while meeting in private homes for common meals, instruction, prayer, and 'fellowship' (2: 42, 46).

The Hellenists

Popular indignation seems to have been provoked by the attitude towards the law exhibited by a group within the Jerusalem community known as 'the Hellenists'. These were Christian Jews who, in contrast to 'the Hebrews', preferred to use the Greek language. Stephen, a member of this group (Acts 6: 1, 5), was accused of speaking 'against this holy place and the law' (6: 14), and his defence does, in fact, include a sharp criticism of the temple cult (7: 47-50). His martyrdom at the hands of an angry mob (7: 57-60) set off a general persecution, which resulted in the dispersal of the Hellenists 'throughout the region of Judaea and Samaria' (Acts 8: 1).

Curiously enough, 'the apostles', i.e. the Twelve, were not affected by this persecution (Acts 8: 1), even though the preaching of their spokesmen, Peter and John, had drawn the ire of the Sadducees. Thus despite the edifying comment that the members of the Jerusalem community 'were of one heart and soul' (Acts 4: 32), the two groups out of which it was composed (6: 1) seem to have had significant differences concerning the binding force of Jewish law, which must have had a divisive effect.

The dispersal of the Hellenists was the occasion for the evangelization of the Samaritans (Acts 8: 4-7). The Jews and the Samaritans were not on friendly terms (cf. John 4: 9), and only persons who felt free from strict Jewish standards could have missionized in Samaria. On the other hand, the two groups shared a common history and a common faith, and it is possible that Jesus concerned himself with the Samaritans (cf. Luke 10: 30-7). At any event, Philip's extension of the mission to Israel to include them was initiated without any previous approval from the Jerusalem authorities.

Technically speaking, since Deut. 23: 1 excludes eunuchs from proselyte status, the first Gentile convert made by one of the Hellenists was the Ethiopian minister baptized by Philip (Acts 8: 38). However, the eunuch's association with Judaism is strongly emphasized in the story (vv. 27-8), and the beginnings of a Gentile mission by the Hellenists are connected with the city of Antioch: 'there were some of [those who were scattered because of the persecution], men of Cyprus and Cyrene, who on coming to Antioch, spoke to the Greeks also, preaching the Lord Jesus' (Acts 11: 20; cf. v. 19). The term 'Greeks' is commonly used in the New Testament to designate Gentiles, i.e. non-Jews. The Hellenists' use of the Greek language and their liberal attitude towards the Torah explains both the possibility and the success of this missionary initiative. However, to the Hebrew party in Jerusalem, which shared the eschatological expectations of the Old Testament, such zeal must have seemed an invasion of what God had reserved for himself. For the pilgrimage of the nations to

Jerusalem (Isa. 2: 2-3) and their share in the eschatological banquet (Isa. 25: 61) were not to be the result of human activity. God would bring the Gentiles in (e.g. Isa. 19: 21), once Israel had been converted. The Hebrews and the Hellenists were at odds not only in the matter of observance of the law but also in their theology and missionary strategy.

The activity of the Hellenists must be seen against the background of Judaism's special position in the Roman Empire. In a period in which the cult of the ancient Greek and Roman deities was more a matter of official state practice than of personal conviction, the religious monotheism and lofty ethical standards of Judaism drew much admiration. Moreover, the Jewish synagogue exercised an unintended power of attraction. The Jewish philosopher, Philo of Alexandria, who lived during the first century CE, was highly regarded and occupied positions of importance. But in spite of Judaism's advantages, the kosher laws and other practices isolated Jews from the general population, and their tendency to separatism occasioned anti-Jewish feeling which sometimes took on violent forms. Nevertheless, many Gentiles sought some form of association with Jewish life and worship.

From the Jewish standpoint, at least in Palestine and probably in the diaspora as well, the object was full conversion, including circumcision and proselyte baptism. Relatively few Gentiles were willing to go this far, not only because accepting the full burden of the law would isolate them from non-Jews, but also because the rite of circumcision, when performed on adults under conditions of ancient hygiene, could be dangerous, as well as painful. Most were content with the ambiguous state of 'God fearers' or 'friends of the synagogue' (cf. Luke 7: 15). Indeed, the term 'Greeks' found in Acts 11: 20 was sometimes used to designate this class of persons (Acts 14: 1; 18: 4; 19: 10).

Peter, James, and Paul

The centurion Cornelius from Caesarea was a 'God fearer' (Acts 10: 2), and Peter's decision to baptize him and his household parallels the missionary activity of the Hellenists in Antioch. However, the admission of such Gentile converts, without circumcision, would remain a matter of controversy until the definitive break between church and synagogue. Indeed, if Christian Jews were the eschatological remnant of Israel, it was difficult to see how someone could share in God's promise of salvation without first being incorporated into his chosen people.

There is no reason to doubt that the Jerusalem community required the circumcision of converted Gentiles. After the dispersal of the Hellenists and the beginning of their missionary activity outside Jerusalem, the Hebrews would have dominated the community. Moreover, following the departure of Peter from the holy city (Acts 12: 17), James, the brother of Jesus, assumed the position of leadership within the community (Acts 21: 18; cf. 12: 17), which further strengthened a conservative direction.

As a follower of Jesus during his earthly ministry, Peter was familar both with criticism of Jewish legalism and with the practice of table-fellowship with non-observant Jews. James, on the contrary, had not been one of Jesus' disciples (Mark 3: 21; John 7: 5), and this difference would explain his rigorism in the matter of table-fellowship with Gentile converts (Gal. 2: 12). The liberal attitude of the Hellenists attracted Gentiles who were eager to exchange their dubious status as 'God fearers' for full membership in the church through baptism. However, to observant Jews the practice of the Hellenists must have looked like apostasy from God's law.

Although Paul had no role in the initial movement of the gospel 'from Jerusalem' (Rom. 15: 19), it was he who would go down in history as the 'apostle to the Gentiles' (Rom. 11: 13). Not only did his prodigious missionary achievements eclipse those of his predecessors; he also undergirded the liberal practice initiated by Peter and the Hellenists with a theological rationale which, in the hindsight of history, has proved to be the sharp end of the wedge which eventually led to two separate religious systems.

Referring to the change brought about by his conversion, Paul writes: 'whatever gain I had, I counted as loss for the sake of Christ. . . . For his sake I have suffered the loss of all things and count them as refuse' (Phil. 3: 8). Clearly, the Damascus experience resulted in a radical reversal of values. This is best illustrated by the change in Paul's attitude towards God's gift to Israel, the Torah.

In the passage just cited Paul declares, in three parallel affirmations, that he was 'as to the law a Pharisee, as to zeal a persecutor of the church [cf. 1 Cor. 15: 9], as to righteousness under the law blameless' (Phil. 3: 5-6). It was as a zealous Pharisaic defender of the Jewish law as the way of righteousness that Paul 'persecuted the church of God violently and tried to destroy it' (Gal. 1: 13). Not the confession of Jesus as the Messiah but rather a blasphemous attitude and practice with regard to the law aroused his ire, just as it had provoked the Jews in Jerusalem against Stephen and the Hellenists.

Paul's view of Israel

Paul's conversion did not lead him simply to adopt the *practice* of the Hellenists in declining to observe the law or to impose it on converts. Having discovered the righteousness which comes through faith in Christ, Paul now regarded the Jewish law as 'refuse', indeed as demonic. Christ had taken upon himself the curse of the law, in order to redeem us from its power (Gal. 3: 13).

Since the Torah contained the divine promise to Abraham which Paul saw fulfilled in Christ (e.g. Rom. 4: 3, 13; cf. Gen. 15: 6), he had to allow that the law, in itself, is 'holy, just, and good' (Rom. 7: 12). But, paradoxically, as soon as fallen man seeks to carry out the law's requirements, he falls victim to sinful boasting in the works of the law, so that 'the very commandment which promised life proved to be death' (Rom. 7: 10).

Paul's rejection of the heart of Jewish teaching and practice inevitably led to a radically new way of viewing God's relations with Israel. Despite his attempt to find some 'advantage' in being a Jew (Rom. 3: 1-2), Paul's substitution of righteousness through faith in place of righteousness through the works of the law meant that Jew and Gentile, apart from Christ, were in exactly the same desperate plight. 'All who have sinned without the law will also perish without the law, and all who have sinned under the law will be judged by the law' (Rom. 2:12). Jews and Gentiles alike 'have *all* sinned and fall short of the glory of God' (Rom. 3: 23). Israel, as an empirical historical reality, has no saving significance. The continuity of salvation history is verified solely at the transcendent level, in God's fidelity to his promises.

Paul's universalization of his own conversion experience produced a theology which was quite incompatible with Jewish self-understanding up to that time. Yet Paul had history on his side, since faith in Christ was to find acceptance mainly outside Israel, among Gentiles, for whom the Jewish law was not sacred and an empirical continuity between Israel and the church was unnecessary.

After 70, the temple lay in ruins, so that much of the law could no longer be observed, and Jews, after their national catastrophe, were moving back to a particularism which would seek to close itself off from Greek influences. Religious Gentiles were interested not in a continuation of Israelite monotheism but in something which could take its place. The new faith would appeal to those who came no longer from 'the friends of the synagogue', but from the myriad cults of the Graeco-Roman world. Paul's proclamation of Christ as Son of God would take on new significance in the context of the mystery religions, in which the cult of a divine saviour played an important role.

Paul himself, however, was far removed from any such vision of the future. Despite his radical break with Jewish religious experience and understanding, he paradoxically sees his gospel as leading to Israel's conversion. The purpose of his mission to Gentiles is to make Israel jealous (Rom. 11: 11). In this extraordinary idea we see how much, in spite of everything, Paul remained a Jew, and how far history outstripped his own aims and expectations.

Paul in the Acts of the Apostles

For Paul's theology we are, of course, entirely dependent upon his own writings. But for his life and interaction with others we have a second source, the book of Acts. The historical value of Acts, in this, as in other matters, is hotly debated. Some aspects of its portrayal of Paul must be rejected, because they conflict with what we know of the historical situation of the period. For example, the author declares that when Paul went to Damascus, to arrest those 'belonging to the Way' (Acts 9: 2), he received letters of authorization from the high-priest in Jerusalem (v. 1). In fact, the Sanhedrin never possessed such authority over communities outside Judaea during the period of Roman administration.

It is also undeniable that the author of Acts pursues a discernible theological purpose in his description of the early church. In particular, his portrait of Paul, which is the one familiar to most people to this day, is more in keeping with 'main-line Christianity' than the idiosyncratic figure who appears to us in the letters. Nevertheless, Luke had good source material at his disposal, even though it cannot easily be isolated within his completed work, and he carries out his theological purpose not through sheer invention but rather by the way in which he combines his sources, for example, in subordinating the mission of the Hellenists to the apostolic initiative of Peter, who, in turn, obeys a direct divine intervention (Acts 10).

In case of a conflict between Acts and Paul's letters, it might seem that the latter, coming from a participant in the story, have a presumption of reliability. Nevertheless, it would be naïve to suppose that Paul's presentation, when he is writing, as so often, under direct personal attack, is either neutral or entirely objective. Both Acts and the Pauline letters must be used in reconstructing Paul's life, and, in the last analysis, the judgement of the modern historian is indispensible.

Paul and Jerusalem

From Paul's letters we know that he made three journeys to Jerusalem. The first occurred three years after his conversion, and its purpose was 'to visit Cephas [Peter]' (Gal. 1: 18). The second visit occurred fourteen years later (Gal. 2: 1) and included a meeting with the 'pillars' of the Jerusalem community (Gal. 2: 9). This meeting is connected in some way with the so-called 'apostles' council' (Acts 15: 1–29), although there are significant differences between the two accounts. Finally, in writing to the Romans, Paul declares his intent to go to Jerusalem to deliver personally the money he had raised for the community there (Rom. 15: 25). This final visit, which led to his arrest, is narrated in Acts 21. Acts also mentions a collection for Jerusalem, but in another connection (11: 27-30).

Although Paul's third and final visit to Jerusalem led to his trial, his journey to Rome, and his martyrdom, it is the second visit which has attracted the special attention of historians, since it gives us a unique insight into the tensions which, less than twenty years after Jesus' crucifixion, were already affecting the new movement.

Later Paul recalls these events in the context of the situation in Galatia, where, once again, he saw his missionary labours threatened with subversion and possible destruction. In defending his position to the Galatians Paul appeals to the discussions in Jerusalem, which had taken place at least five years before, with persons with whom he never enjoyed a relationship of mutual confidence or intimacy. We must therefore be on our guard against assuming that Paul's recollection of his agreement with James, Peter, and John represents the understanding of all the participants.

The extremely limited nature of Paul's agreement with the Jerusalem authorities is indicated by the fact that Paul himself expresses it in terms of a *separation* between two spheres of missionary activity: 'we [Paul and Barnabas] should go to the Gentiles and they [James, Peter, and John] to the circumcised' (Gal. 2: 9). Neither the theological problem of the law as a way of salvation nor the practical problem of social and religious intercourse between Jews and non-Jews seems to have been discussed.

The Jerusalem authorities were evidently impressed by the success of Paul's missionary activity: 'when they saw that I had been entrusted with the gospel to the uncircumcized' (Gal. 2: 7); 'when they perceived the grace that was given to me' (v. 9). But Paul does not tell us how the Jerusalem leaders viewed his missionary labours in relation to their own.

However, in the Lucan account of the 'apostles' council' we find a formulation which may reflect Jerusalem's understanding of the two separate missions. 'After they [Barnabas and Paul] had finished speaking, James replied, "Brethren, listen to me. Simeon [i.e. Peter] has related how God first visited the Gentiles [cf. Acts 10], to take out of them a people for his name"' (Acts 15: 13-14). There follows a scriptural proof-text (Amos 9: 11-12), in which the rebuilding of the fallen dwelling of David has consequences for 'all the nations'.

James declares that God's eschatological renewal of his covenant with Israel through the death and resurrection of Jesus has led 'the rest of men to seek the Lord' (Acts 15: 17). The 'expectant universalism' of the Old Testament, which was shared by Jesus himself (Matt. 8: 11 par.), is in the process of being fulfilled. Here we have a conception which is quite different from Paul's vision of one people of God, made up of Jews and Gentiles (Rom. 15: 7-13). For James, Israel is still God's chosen people and hence still bound by the law which God had given them.

However, God has now seen fit to visit the Gentiles, in order to make out of them *another* people for his name. *Two* eschatological communities have thus come into being: the remnant of Israel and a new people, who share in Israel's monotheistic faith and in the confession of Jesus as the Messiah, but are not subject to the law and therefore not obliged to undergo circumcision. A theological rationale had been found for the Gentile mission begun by the Hellenists and now pursued with such evident success by Paul.

The decision of the Jerusalem authorities to reject the demand that Paul's Gentile converts be circumcized (Acts 15: 1; Gal. 2: 3-4) was doubtless welcome to him, but James's reason for his decision was entirely incompatible with Paul's theological radicalism. According to the agreement, the law remained the way of salvation for Israel, and Paul's inability to accept this position led to further controversy.

The continuing validity of the law for Jews found concrete expression in their refusal to share common meals with Gentiles, who did not observe the kosher laws. This practice led to difficulties in the community in Antioch, which, ever since the Hellenists' initiative, had been made up of Jewish and Gentile converts.

Peter's response to this problem was pragmatic. He seems to have regarded the law as adaptable to particular circumstances, and he declined to accept either the rigorism of James or Paul's hostile rejection of the law. Consequently, though he had no personal scruples about eating with Gentiles (Gal. 2: 12), he did respect the weak conscience of those who took a different position, just as Paul himself would do in similar circumstances (1 Cor. 8: 9-13; Rom. 14: 1-4). So when 'certain men came [to Antioch] from James', i.e. from the Jerusalem community, Peter 'drew back and separated himself' (Gal. 2: 12), not 'because he feared the circumcision party', as Paul uncharitably assumes, but in order not to give scandal (cf. 1 Cor. 8: 13; Rom. 14: 21).

Peter's action sparked a violent denunciation by Paul, which brought out into the open the deep theological gulf which existed not only between Paul and James, but even between Paul and moderates such as Peter and Barnabas. But Paul's impassioned accusation that Peter was hypocritically attempting to force Gentiles to abide by Jewish prescriptions which he himself did not observe (Gal. 2: 14) really reflects what *Paul* was trying to do, namely, to force Jews to live as Gentiles by sharing table-fellowship with Gentile converts.

Paul is unable to report to the Galatians that either Peter or Barnabas—Paul's former missionary associate—came around to his position. In fact, the consequence of this altercation was that Paul left Antioch for good, except for the brief visit mentioned in Acts 18: 22-3, in order to resume independent missionary activity. The episode also seems to have led to worsening relations between Paul and the Jerusalem community.

The breakdown of the Jerusalem agreement in Antioch appears to have moved James to regulate more strictly the relations between Christian Jews and Gentiles in the province under his control. This is the effect of his letter to Gentile Christians living in Antioch, Syria, and Cilicia (Acts 15: 23). Although this decree appears in Acts as the result of the 'apostles' council', it was clearly issued at a later date, since James has to inform Paul about it when the latter arrives in Jerusalem for his final visit (Acts 21: 25).

The four prohibitions contained in this decree (Acts 15: 29) recall the four things proscribed by the Holiness Code (Lev. 17-18) not only for 'any man of the house of Israel' but also for 'the strangers that sojourn among them' (Lev. 17: 8). There is no reason to suppose that the decree intends to facilitate any closer intimacy between Jews and Gentiles than the prescriptions of the Holiness Code itself. It certainly does not authorize the illicit table-fellowship which was practised at Antioch before the arrival of James's delegation (Gal. 2: 12). On the contrary, the four requirements are imposed on Gentile Christians as a condition for their living in the same locality as Jews. They represent a toughening of the position of the Jerusalem authorities, in contrast with the agreement at the 'apostles' council', when, according to Paul, 'they imposed no additional obligation upon me' (Gal. 2: 6) [author's translation].

These developments explain how it could happen that, despite the agreement reached at the 'apostle's council', missionaries arrived in Galatia to circumcise Paul's Gentile converts (Gal. 5: 2-3). Although these persons need not have come from Jerusalem, it is doubtful whether, after the Antioch episode, the Jerusalem authorities continued in their support of Paul's missionary venture. If he felt free to encourage Jews to break the law (cf. Acts 21: 21), why should they prohibit his converts from being incorporated into God's chosen people through circumcision?

Paul's ambivalence towards the Jerusalem community finds expression in the last recorded words of his that we possess. Writing to the Romans, he refers to the final task which he must perform before leaving the East for Rome and Spain: 'I am going to Jerusalem with aid for the saints' (Rom. 15: 25). He awaits this journey with trepidation, as is clear from his urgent appeal for prayers (v. 30). Significantly, his fears concern both 'the unbelievers in Judaea' (i.e. non-Christian Jews), and the Jerusalem community, whose acceptance of Paul's gift is far from certain (v. 31). Would this financial assistance for the poor, which the Jerusalem authorities had requested at the 'apostles' council' and which Paul had been so eager to give (Gal. 2: 10), still be welcome after what had happened in between? We do not know the answer to this question. However, it is surely significant that when Paul was arrested in the holy city (Acts 21: 33) at the instigation of 'Jews from Asia' (v. 27), the Jerusalem community did not come to his assistance.

Paul's attitude towards this community parallels his attitude to his fellow Jews generally. Just as Israel has 'the sonship, the glory, the covenants, the giving of the law, the worship, and the promise' (Rom. 9: 4), so Jerusalem is the source of the 'spiritual blessings' which 'the Gentiles have come to share' (Rom. 15: 27; cf. 11: 18).

For Paul, the collection was more than a means of securing Jerusalem's non-interference in his missionary endeavours. It was also an expression of his deep veneration for the holy city. The confession of faith in Jesus' death and resurrection (1 Cor. 15: 3-4), which Paul himself had 'received' and which he, in turn, 'delivered' to the Corinthians 'as of first importance', probably came from the Jerusalem community.

Nevertheless, Paul's conversion did not simply make him a Jew who believed that Jesus was the Messiah. If Jews continued to observe the law after being converted to Christ, he had no objection. Indeed, he writes, 'To the Jews I became as a Jew, in order to win Jews' (1 Cor. 9: 20). But to attribute to such practices any saving significance or to allow them to become a barrier between Jews and believing Gentiles was utterly intolerable, as his outburst in Antioch made clear. His insistence that justification by the law means separation from Christ (Gal. 5: 4) applies as much to the Jerusalem community as to the 'foolish Galatians' (Gal. 3: 1). This uncompromising 'either-or' not only made impossible any real co-operation with Jerusalem; it also pointed ahead to the definitive separation of Christianity from the parent faith.

Matthew's special material

Christian Jews who were living in Palestine before the outbreak of the Jewish War, under the leadership of the Jerusalem community, had no reason to become involved in a mission to Gentiles. The pluralism of pre-war Judaism permitted them to exist as one group among many, even if it did not exempt them from all harassment, especially at the hands of the Sadducees. On the other hand, the Gentile mission was increasingly dominated by the theological radicalism of Paul, which relegated the observance of the law to the status of optional ethnic custom.

However, this situation changed radically as a result of the war and the changes which it produced, both within Judaism and within Jewish Christianity. We are able to trace this development in Matthew's gospel, particularly in the special material which it contains. This material, which is not found in either of the other synoptic gospels, is composed of two distinct and sometimes contradictory elements. On the one hand, we have the special *tradition* of the Matthean community, which has more parallels with rabbinic Judaism than any other gospel tradition. On the other hand, we have the *redaction* of the author of the gospel, whose Gentile origins are indicated by the fact that he has made the Gentile gospel of Mark the basis for his own composition.

In our reading of Matthew's gospel, we shall be adopting an approach which may seem novel and perhaps even dubious to those accustomed to reading this book as a collection of traditions about the teaching and actions of Jesus. Such a traditional approach to the work is in no way negated by seeking to read between the lines the history of the community to which the evangelist is writing. All the gospels must be read on two levels, as narratives of the ministry of Jesus and as reflections of the ecclesiastical contexts in which and for which they were written. Only in recent decades, with the development of redaction criticism, has this second way of reading the gospels been brought to bear on the historical reconstruction of Christianity from about 60 to 90 CE. Like any tool, redaction criticism is only as good as the judgement of the scholar who is using it. In what follows we are moving beyond the present scholarly consensus, and the reader must make his own judgement on the plausibility of our reconstruction.

The saying in Matt. 10: 23, found only in this gospel, points to Palestine as the place of origin of the community: 'when they persecute you in one town, flee to the next; for truly, I say to you, you will not have gone through all the towns of Israel, before the Son of man comes'. In the original sense of this instruction, 'the cities of Israel' must be understood geographically, as the parallel expression, 'the land of Israel' (Matt. 2: 20-1), makes clear. But a restriction of the community's mission to Palestine presupposes that the community itself is located there. The special material involving temple sacrifice (5: 23-4) and the temple tax (17: 24-7) points in the same direction.

Matthew's special tradition includes an affirmation of the unconditional validity of the entire Torah: 'whoever relaxes one of the least of these commandments and teaches men so, shall be called least in the kingdom of heaven; but he who does them and teaches them shall be called great in the kingdom of heaven' (5: 19). This categorical pronouncement is reinforced by a saying which Matthew shares with Luke, but which is more severe in its Matthean form: 'for truly, I say to you, till heaven and earth pass away, not an iota, not a dot, will pass from the law until all is accomplished' (5: 18; cf. Luke 16: 17). The community's fidelity to the law is combined with obedience to Pharisaic teaching. While the conduct of the Pharisees is criticized, as inconsistent with their teaching, the community is none the less commanded: 'practise and observe whatever they tell you' (Matt. 23: 2).

Coupled with this legalistic rigorism and flowing from it as a necessary consequence is a prohibition against missionizing Gentiles or Samaritans: 'go nowhere among the Gentiles, and enter no town of the Samaritans, but go rather to the lost sheep of the house of Israel' (Matt. 10: 5-6). The missionary activity of the Hellenists is off limits for the Matthean community. However, in the same chapter of the gospel, we find Jesus alluding to a mission to Gentiles. He warns 'his twelve disciples' (10: 1): 'beware of men; for they will deliver you up to councils, and flog you in their synagogues, and you will be dragged before governors and kings for my sake, as a testimony for them *and the Gentiles*' (vv. 17-18; author's translation of the concluding phrase). The expression used here can have a negative significance, i.e. 'for a testimony *against* them' (Mark 6: 11). However in the context of Jesus' discourse, which emphasizes the parallelism between himself and his missionary disciples, the latter's suffering appears to serve as a witness *for the benefit* of the two groups mentioned: the Jews, in whose synagogues the disciples will be flogged, and the Gentiles. Both groups are beneficiaries of the witness which the disciples give *through their suffering*, even though the disciples' *preaching* mission is limited to Israel alone (10: 5b-6, 23).

The Matthean community is therefore aware of the *existence* of a Gentile mission, even though they are excluded from direct participation in it. In this implication of two separate missions, Matt. 10 recalls the agreement reached at the 'apostles' council' (Gal. 2: 8-9).

The slurring references to Gentiles in Matthew's gospel attest to the Jewish particularism of the Matthean community. The Gentiles appear as an example of how *not* to act: 'in praying do not heap up empty phrases as the Gentiles do' (6: 7); 'the Gentiles seek all these things [i.e. material goods, such as food, drink, and clothing]' (6: 32; cf. 5: 47). Indeed, the term 'Gentile' is combined, in an excommunication formula, with the hated 'publican', who contracted with the Roman authorities to gather taxes, at a profit to himself (18: 17).

The Matthean community and the Jewish War

The sufferings of the Jewish War intensified these sentiments. The persecution which the community suffered earlier in Jewish councils and synagogues (Matt. 10: 17) is now inflicted by Gentiles: 'then they will deliver you up to tribulation, and put you to death; and you will be hated by all the Gentiles for my name's sake' (Matt. 24: 9). During this period the Gentiles will deliver up the Matthean community to a tribulation which is associated with 'the great tribulation' (v. 21) of the Jewish War itself. During this catastrophe of the Jewish nation, Matthew's community of Christian Jews shared the suffering of non-Christian Jews, enduring it for the sake of the name of Christ.

Also connected with the Jewish War is an upheaval *within* the Matthean community: 'and then many will fall away, and betray one another, and hate one another' (v. 10). The internecine strife which afflicted Jews during the war and was later judged by the rabbis to be the reason why God allowed the temple to be destroyed also affected Matthew's community of Christian Jews. But the factionalism within his community was not over political issues. It involved apostasy from the law: 'many will fall away' (Matt. 24: 10); 'lawlessness is multiplied' (v. 12; author's translation). Who was responsible for this development? We are told that 'many false prophets will arise and lead many astray' (v. 11). Matthew recalls that during the Jewish War many within his community, seduced by false prophets, apostatized from Judaism, in order to escape persecution at the hands of the Gentiles.

Matthew alludes cryptically to the result of this development: 'because lawlessness is multiplied, love for the many will grow cold' (v. 12) [author's translation]. 'The many' for whose forgiveness Christ shed his blood (Matt. 26: 28), in fulfilment of the fourth

'Servant Song' (Isa. 53: 12), are none other than the Gentiles (cf.
Matt. 12: 18, 21 = Isa. 42: 1, 4). Matthew's community, as the true
Israel, is called to be 'the light of the world' (Matt. 5: 14). However,
because of the persecution inflicted by the Gentiles during the
Jewish War and the apostasy from the law to which this led, the dis-
like for Gentiles reflected in Matthew's special tradition has turned
to hatred.

Eusebius informs us that the Jerusalem community was able to
escape the doomed city before the Roman siege began (*EH* III.v.3).
Matthew's community, wherever in Palestine they may have been
located, appears to have participated in the exodus. For the evangelist, some of the prophecies in Mark's gospel have now been
fulfilled: 'when you see the desolating sacrilege [*or* "sacrilegious
desolation"] spoken of by the prophet Daniel, standing in the holy
place (let the reader understand), then let those who are in Judaea
flee to the mountains' (Matt. 24: 15-16). Writing after 70, Matthew
refers clearly to the destruction of the temple (contrast Mark 13: 14).
This event was the sign for the Matthean community to flee Judaea.

The Matthean community in Syria

Clearly the community had settled in a Greek-speaking area by the
time the gospel was written. Besides the language of the gospel itself, the fact that Matthew refers to Daniel as 'the prophet' (24:
15) indicates that his community was using the Greek Bible, in
which the book of Daniel is included among 'the prophets', and
not among 'the writings', as in the Hebrew Bible.

The actual home of the community after their flight from Palestine may be alluded to in Matt. 4: 24. This verse contains the only
reference to Syria in the gospels, apart from Luke 2: 2. After men-
tionining Jesus' preaching and teaching journey in Galilee and the
healings that he performed 'among the people' (Matt. 4: 23), Matthew
adds: 'so his fame spread throughout all Syria' (v. 24). Thus a
connection is established between Jesus' ministry, which was for
the benefit of 'the people', i.e. Israel (cf. 15: 24), and the area in
which the Matthean community is likely to have settled.

Syria was the area where Gentile Christianity had begun, and
by the year 70 it must have obtained a firm foothold there. The

movement of the Matthean community beyond the boundaries of Palestine was a precondition for a new relationship to non-Jews and to Gentile Christianity. In a prophecy found, in this form, only in Matthew's gospel, we read: 'this gospel of the kingdom will be preached throughout the whole world, as a testimony to all the Gentiles' (Matt. 24: 14) (RSV has 'all nations'). More explicitly than in Matt. 10: 18, the evangelist affirms the existence of a worldwide mission which will be for the benefit of Gentiles; the Jews are no longer mentioned. However, his community is still not directly engaged in preaching to Gentiles.

The Matthean community and post-70 Pharisaism

The events of the year 70 had other consequences besides the geographical displacement of the Matthean community. The centre of Jewish worship, the temple, was in ruins, and the centre of Jewish Christianity, the Jerusalem community, had left the holy city. Non-Christian Judaism made a new beginning under the leadership of Yochanan ben Zakkai, who had opposed the use of violent means to achieve national liberation. Two years before the end of the war, he had obtained, from the Roman commander Vespasian, permission to found a school in Jamnia, on the coast of Palestine.

In post-70 Judaism, under the leadership of the Pharisees, we find a tendency towards uniformity which demanded more than merely halakic conformism (the observance of the *practical* obligations of the law). This development made the position of Christian Jews increasingly difficult. Jews seem to have been prohibited from associating with the Nazarenes, and the bitter polemic against Pharisaism, which permeates Matthew's gospel, points to the tragic predicament of the community.

The references to '*their* synagogue[s]' (Matt. 4: 23; 9: 35; 10: 17; 12: 9; 13: 54) and to '*your* synagogues' (23: 34) (when the Pharisees are addressed) indicate that Matthew's community was holding separate religious assemblies. The community was vilified (5: 11), slandered (12: 7), and subjected to active persecution (5: 10-12, 44; 10: 23; 23: 34). The reference to the crucifixion of community members at the hands of the scribes and Pharisees (Matt. 23: 34) has been dismissed as unhistorical, on the grounds that the Jews did not have the legal authority to inflict capital punishment (John 18: 31). However, this does not rule out illegal acts, such as the stoning of Stephen (Acts 7: 57-9) or the execution of James, the Lord's brother (Josephus, *Ant.* xx. 200). Moreover, two Qumran texts, 4QpNah and 11QTemple, apparently refer to crucifixion, which would seem to imply that not only the Romans had made use of this mode of punishment. It is not impossible, therefore, that members of Matthew's community had actually been crucified by other Jews.

Jerusalem's murder of the Old Testament prophets is followed by the rejection and murder of Jesus himself (23: 37; 21: 39) and the persecution of his emissaries: 'therefore I send you prophets and wise men and scribes, some of whom you will kill and crucify, and some you will scourge in your synagogues and persecute from town to town, that upon you may come all the righteous blood shed on earth' (23: 34-5).

The evangelist's hostility to the scribes and Pharisees makes clear that persecution was a present reality for his readers and not simply a piece of past history. The Matthean Jesus solemnly announces that 'all this'—the crimes mentioned in the preceding verses—'will come upon this generation' (Matt. 23: 36). In the destruction of the Jerusalem temple (24: 2) the evangelist sees the divine retribution (cf. 21: 41) for the persecution of the prophets which has culminated in the suffering of his community.

The Matthean community and the Gentile mission

If the Gentile mission became an option for the Matthean community only after their resettlement in Syria after the Jewish War, the motivation to embrace this option is to be seen in the increasingly negative stance of post-war Judaism towards Jewish Christianity. The evangelist is clearly in favour of moving in the direction of the Gentile mission, since he closes his gospel with a command from the risen Lord: 'go therefore and make disciples of all the Gentiles' (RSV reads 'all nations') (28: 19). Since Israel is a 'nation', Jews are not excluded from this univeral mandate. However, with God's judgement against Jerusalem in the city's destruction by the Romans, the special mission to Israel (10: 5b-6, 23) is terminated.

To many in Matthew's community the fierce persecution which

they were now suffering from Jewish leaders must have put the conversion of Israel beyond the realm of possibility, so that participation in the Gentile mission became overpoweringly attractive. To others, however, it must have seemed a temptation to apostasy, born of desperation. In any case, Matthew's gospel gives us an insight into a community of Christian Jews which has been polarized by this controversial issue. A major purpose of the book seems to have been a reconciliation between the community's Jewish past and present calling, which would enable it to embark on the task which historical developments were indicating.

'The Gospel of Signs'

Just as Matthew's gospel is a revision of the Gospel of Mark, so the fourth and latest of the canonical gospels, attributed by tradition to John, represents a new edition of an earlier work, called 'The Gospel of Signs', because it centres upon seven miracles of Jesus. There is extensive scholarly agreement that the Fourth Evangelist has used such a document, even though its reconstruction remains a matter of some debate.

Like Matthew's special tradition, the 'Gospel of Signs' comes from a community of Christian Jews, which is quite at home within Judaism. It shows no concern for the Gentile question and takes for granted the observance of the Torah. Through Andrew, the first disciple to be called, the reader learns: 'we have found the Messiah' (John 1: 41). Philip informs Nathanael that 'Jesus of Nazareth, the son of Joseph', is the one 'of whom Moses in the law and the prophets also wrote' (v. 45). On the other hand, the expectation which we find in the synoptic tradition of Jesus returning in judgement as the Son of man is notably absent. Indeed, the 'Gospel of Signs' shows little apocalyptic influence of any kind.

The Johannine community and post-70 Judaism

The revision of the 'Gospel of Signs' by the Fourth Evangelist was occasioned by a traumatic experience in the life of his community:

its expulsion from the synagogue. The memory of this event is preserved in the story of the man born blind: 'the Jews had agreed that if anyone should confess [Jesus] to be Christ, he was to be put out of the synagogue' (John 9: 22). When the man born blind persists in his assertion that Jesus has come from God (v. 33), despite his having healed him on the sabbath, '[the Jews] cast him out' (v. 34).

This exclusion from the synagogue is thought to have been effected by the inclusion of 'the Nazarenes' in 'the blessing of the heretics'—the twelfth petition in the Prayer of Eighteen Petitions, which was recited as a regular part of the synagogue service: 'for apostates let there be no hope, and the dominion of arrogance do thou speedily root out in our days, and let Nazarenes and heretics perish as in a moment; let them be blotted out of the book of the living and let them not be written with the righteous. Blessed art thou, O Lord, who humblest the arrogant' (b.Ber. 28b).

This form of the petition, which was introduced around the year 85, made it impossible for members of the Johannine community to attend the synagogue service without invoking a curse on their own heads. After this action by the Pharisaic leadership, some members of the Johannine community decided to stay safely within the synagogue. Those who remained openly loyal to their confession of Jesus as the Christ became a separate community. Their alienation from the majority of their fellow Jews led them to new christological formulations. Instead of Jesus being portrayed as the fulfilment of Jewish expectations, he is now presented as the Stranger from above (John 8: 23), 'who came to his own home, but his own people did not receive him' (1: 11; author's translation).

Such formulations exposed the Johannine community to the charge of ditheism, making Jesus into a second God: 'this is why the Jews sought all the more to kill [Jesus], because he not only broke the sabbath but also called God his own Father, making himself equal with God' (5: 18). The Johannine Christ does not hesitate to use the name revealed by God to Moses at Sinai, 'Say this to the people of Israel', "I AM has sent me to you"' (Exod. 3: 14). In the Fourth Gospel Jesus declares to 'the Jews' (John 8: 48), 'Truly, truly, I say to you, before Abraham was, I am' (v. 58).

The Johannine community and other Christian groups

The community's high christology made them suspicious of other Christian groups, which had not undergone the same development. Crypto-Christians, who conceal their belief in Christ (like Nicodemus (3: 1-2) and Joseph of Arimathea (19: 38)), in order to remain in the synagogue, are no better than 'the Jews' themselves: 'they loved the praise of men more than the praise of God' (12: 43).

Another suspect group may be indicated by the 'many' who 'believed in [Jesus'] name, when he was in Jerusalem at the Passover feast, when they saw the signs which he did' (2: 23). Jesus' response reflects the evangelist's own disapproval: 'he did not trust himself to them, because he knew all men and needed no one to bear witness of man; for he himself knew what was in man' (vv. 24-5).

This hostility to believers in Jerusalem may take on historical significance when combined with the reference to Jesus' unbelieving brothers (7: 5). For among these brothers was James (Mark 6: 3 par.), the leader of the Jerusalem community. Despite the fact that James had died a martyr's death by the time that the Fourth Evangelist was writing, Jesus' brothers are never represented in a favourable light in the gospel. The Christians in Jerusalem, for whom the evangelist expresses his aversion, may therefore be followers of James.

The Fourth Evangelist's relationship to the form of Christianity contained in Matthew's gospel is rather different. This is indicated by his treatment of Peter, who is the subject of three sections in Matthew's special material (Matt. 14: 28-31; 16: 17-19; 17: 24-7; cf. 18: 21 par.). Peter's confession of Jesus as 'the Christ, the Son of the living God' (Matt. 16: 16) does not go as far as the christology of the Johannine community, according to which Jesus is the pre-existent Word of God (John 1: 1). On the contrary, Matthew's gospel reflects a 'conception christology', according to which Jesus' divine sonship is explained by the activity of the spirit at his conception (Matt. 1: 18-25), rather than by a begetting by the Father 'in the beginning' (John 1: 1, 14).

On the other hand, the Fourth Evangelist shows no hostility toward Peter. He has him deliver a confession of faith, after 'many of [Jesus'] disciples drew back and no longer went about with him' (6: 66). In the name of the Twelve (v. 67), Peter says to Jesus: 'Lord, to whom shall we go? You have the words of eternal life; and we have believed, and have come to know that you are the Holy One of God' (vv. 68-9). Moreover, the epilogue to the gospel recalls that Peter had glorified God by his death (21: 19).

Nevertheless, the faith of the Johannine community is represented by the beloved disciple, who is the supreme example of Jesus' 'own' (13: 1). He is closer to Jesus than Peter, both in life and in death. He reclines on Jesus' breast at the Last Supper (13: 23), and he stands by Jesus' cross (19: 26). Moreover, he is the one who perceives the significance of the empty tomb (20: 8) and recognizes the risen Lord (21: 7). In these two scenes Peter and the beloved disciple appear in a competitive relationship which expresses the relationship between the communities which they represent.

Peter and, presumably, the Matthean community which venerated his memory, do not yet share the Fourth Evangelist's knowledge of Jesus' true origin, and the pre-eminence of the beloved disciple relativizes Peter's 'apostolic' authority. Nevertheless, Peter is acknowledged in the epilogue as a shepherd of the sheep (21: 15-17), and this recognition has important ecclesiological implications, as we shall see in our concluding chapter.

The Johannine community may show a sectarian mentality in its claims of a unique closeness of the beloved disciple to Jesus, of a superior understanding of who Jesus is, and of the special guidance of the spirit (16: 13). Nevertheless, it does not appear to deny all fellowship with communities such as the one addressed in Matthew's gospel. It may, in fact, have had such believers in mind when Jesus refers to the 'other sheep I have, that are not of this fold. I must bring them also, and they will heed my voice. So there will be one flock, one shepherd' (10: 16; cf. 17: 21). If so, the prayed-for unity with the 'other sheep' did finally come about. By the time the canon was formed, Christians who used Matthew's gospel also accepted the christology of the Fourth Evangelist and his community, as the presence of both books in the New Testament makes clear.

Conclusion

In the three strands of New Testament tradition which we have considered—Paul and the Matthean and Johannine communities—four issues stand out which are relevant for the emergence of a Christian self-consciousness: 1) freedom from the Torah, 2) christology, 3) the Gentile mission, and 4) Jewish persecution. Taken individually, no one of these would account for the development of the Christian movement into a religion distinct from Judaism.

1. Failure to observe the Jewish law was nothing new in the experience of Israel. In the Hellenistic and Roman periods, such 'apostasy' was motivated by a desire for greater conformity with the prevailing culture, but it did not lead to a new religion.

2. Christology, particularly in the advanced form that we find in the Fourth Gospel, was to become the chief distinguishing mark of Christianity. However, there were Jews who believed that Jesus was the Christ without in any way losing their sense of Jewish identity. On the contrary, this confession was the mark of their membership in the eschatological remnant of Israel, just as an observance of the law which outdid the practice of the Pharisees expressed the conviction of the Qumran community that they were 'the sons of light' in the impending eschatological conflict.

3. Although the Jews did not send out missionaries expressly to proselytize among the heathen, there was a well-developed and effective propaganda movement, particularly in Diaspora Judaism, during the first century CE (cf. Matt. 23: 15; Rom. 2: 19).

4. Persecution of Jews by other Jews, e.g. Pharisaic persecution of the Qumran sectaries, did not necessarily lead to a loss of Jewish identity. However, the theological question of who was 'a real Jew' (cf. Rom. 2: 28) had significant implications, since it raised the issue of who was entitled to the special privileges accorded by Rome to the Jewish people.

It was the convergence of these four factors which seems to have been decisive, and the emergence of a Jewish sect which offered full membership to non-Jews, without requiring circumcision or separation from the dominant culture, was certainly a new phenomenon in the religious landscape (cf. Eph. 2: 12).

The recollection that 'the disciples were called Christians for the first time in Antioch' (Acts 11: 26), the city where some of the Hellenists 'spoke to the Greeks also' (v. 20), expresses the significance of this development. When Paul proclaims that 'Christ is the end of the law' (Rom. 10: 4), he provides a theological rationale for a missionary practice which had already given the initiative of the Hellenists an enormous advantage over other Jewish propaganda efforts.

In this chapter we have laboured under the disadvantage that our main source material has represented the standpoint of the 'winners', i.e. those groups within the Christian movement whose faith and practice were moving them, even without their being aware of it, beyond the bounds of Judaism. The self-understanding of the 'losers', i.e. those primarily concerned with their own Jewish identity and the mission to Israel, is available to us in so far as it has been incorporated into the canonical writings accepted by the Gentile church of the second and third centuries. We have found James's view of the Pauline mission preserved in Luke's account of the 'apostles' council' (Acts 15); the 'special tradition' preserved in Matthew's gospel and the 'Gospel of Signs' have given us glimpses into the history of two communities of Christian Jews.

How did Jesus of Nazareth come to be acclaimed as 'the redeemer of the Gentiles', as in the opening line of Ambrose's hymn (*Veni, redemptor gentium*)? Why did a Jewish sect emerge as the religion of the Roman Empire? The evidence for a complex interaction of a variety of historical factors undermines the 'classical' view of early Christian history as the triumphant advance of a divine revelation, contained in a 'deposit of faith' (cf. 1 Tim. 6: 20; 2 Tim. 1: 12, 14), which was known and accepted from the beginning by all right-minded persons. On the other hand, historical reconstruction does not reduce what finally emerged to a mere quirk of history. To see in the complex skein of historical causality the working out of some higher plan remains a responsible option for the believer, even though it exceeds the limitations of the historian's craft.

6

The Church

From 'the churches' to 'the church'

Today, 'Christianity' and 'the church' are virtually synonymous terms. The latter is used not simply to designate a particular local community of Christian believers but also a fellowship which transcends congregational and even national boundaries.

It therefore comes as a surprise to the contemporary Christian to discover that the use of 'the church' to designate the Christian movement as a whole is a relatively late development within the New Testament literature. As we see from the opening verses of the Pauline letters, the oldest writings in the New Testament, 'the church' is usually specified: 'the church of God which is at Corinth' (1 Cor. 1: 2); 'the churches of Galatia' (Gal. 1: 2); 'the church of the Thessalonians' (1 Thess. 1: 1); 'the church in your [i.e. Philemon's] house' (Philem. 2).

In two places Paul uses 'the church' in the singular in contexts in which it cannot refer to a single congregation. However, in both instances he is summarizing what is true of several local communities. Both 'the church of God' (Gal. 1: 13) and 'the churches in Judaea' (v. 22) have been the object of Paul's destructive zeal before his conversion (cf. v. 23: 'he who once persecuted us'). 'The church of God' seems to be an honorific title for the Jewish-Christian communities in Judaea and Jerusalem, a title which corresponds to the cultic designation of Israel during its wanderings in the wilderness as 'the assembly of the Lord' (Num. 20: 4). Two other occurrences of 'the church of God', 1 Cor. 15: 9 and Phil. 3: 6 (in some manuscripts), refer to the object of Paul's activity as a persecutor and therefore designate these same communities in Judaea and Jerusalem. Another use of 'the church' in the singular has a different explanation: when Paul declares that 'God has appointed in the church first apostles, second prophets, third teachers' (1 Cor. 12: 28), he is describing the structure of all the communities which he has founded.

The understanding of 'the church' as a reality which transcends the limits of both time and space seems to have resulted from cosmological reflection, as well as from the development of a Christian universalism which was no longer satisfied with two separate missions to Jews and to Gentiles (cf. Gal. 2: 8-9). In Paul's letters Christ is identified with the local church, which is his body. He tells the Corinthian community, 'You are the body of Christ' (1 Cor. 12: 27); the head is just one member of the body (v. 21). In Colossians (1: 18; 2: 19) and Ephesians (1: 22; 4: 15), however, Christ is specifically identified as the head of the body. In the latter epistle, the cosmological relationship between the church universal and the exalted Christ is reflected in the marital relationship between husband and wife (Eph. 5: 31-2).

The only gospel in which the word 'church' occurs is the Gospel according to Matthew. In ch. 18 the word is used to designate the local congregation (v. 17 (twice)); in ch. 16 it has a universalist sense (v. 18). A major purpose of Matthew's gospel was to move a congregation marked by Jewish particularism in the direction of the Gentile mission (28: 19). Consequently, the occurrence of the same universalist use of 'church' which we find in Ephesians takes on special significance. The movement away from Judaism towards a broader mission in the Graeco-Roman world was responsible both for a new self-understanding, expressed by the designation 'Christian' (Acts 11: 26), and for universalist and cosmological interpretations of the community structures which the new movement was producing. This development in theological understanding preceded the organizational developments which were to give empirical expression to the idea of the 'one church'.

The apostle as founder

In both Matthew and Ephesians the church has an apostolic 'foundation'. After changing Simon's name to Peter ('rock'), Jesus declares,

'On this rock I will build my church' (Matt. 16: 18). For the author of Ephesians, the church, as 'the household of God' (2: 19), is 'built upon the foundation of the apostles and prophets, Christ himself being the cornerstone' (v. 20).

Many ancient centres of Christianity have laid claim to apostolic foundation. However, from what we learn in Acts about the activity of the Hellenists in Samaria (8: 4-8) and Antioch (11: 19-21), it is clear that the foundation of Christian communities was often the result of spontaneous missionary activity, occasioned in this case by the persecution of the Hellenists (8: 1). No apostolic figure was involved in the initial evangelization, although, in the representation of Acts, the foundation of the two communities was subsequently ratified by Jerusalem, which sent Peter and John to Samaria (8: 14) and Barnabas to Antioch (11: 22).

Christianity in Rome appears to have been the result not of missionary activity but rather of the immigration of Christians from Palestine and Syria, who joined together to form a community. Ambrosiaster (the name given to the author of Latin commentaries, formerly attributed to Ambrose, on the Pauline epistles) is scarcely expressing a private opinion when he declares that the Romans 'accepted faith in Christ without seeing any miraculous works or any apostle' (Prologue to the *Commentary on Romans*). According to early tradition, the apostle Peter is associated with Rome. In the first letter attributed to him, the author sends greetings from the church which is 'at Babylon' (1 Pet. 5: 13), and 'Babylon' is almost certainly a slurring reference to the imperial capital (cf. Rev. 14: 8; 18: 2). However, Peter was certainly not the *founder* of the Roman church, since he is still in Jerusalem for the 'apostles' council' (46/48), by which time the Christians in Rome had become sufficiently numerous for their disputes with non-Christian Jews to occasion the Emperor Claudius to expel all Jews from the city (Suetonius, *Life of Claudius*, ch. 25; cf. Acts 18: 2).

Only in the letters of Paul do we have contemporary testimony to the foundation of churches by an apostle. In a variation of the architectural metaphor, Paul declares to the Corinthians, 'According to the grace of God given to me, like a skilled master builder I laid a foundation' (1 Cor. 3: 10; cf. v. 6). However, the notion of the apostle(s) as founder(s) of Christian communities goes beyond its historical verifiability. It takes on a crucial theological significance in the formation of the New Testament canon and in the use of the word 'apostolic' throughout the history of the Christian church.

'Apostle of Jesus Christ'–'apostles of the churches'

The word 'apostle' is used in the New Testament to designate both the founder of a church and the emissary of a church. In the latter sense, the apostle (Acts 14: 4, 14) is 'sent' by the community, whether to missionary endeavours (Acts 13: 1-3; 2 Cor. 8: 23; cf. Rom. 16: 7) or with a more limited mandate. Epaphroditus is the 'apostle' of the Philippian community (Phil. 2: 25), which has sent him to deliver the church's gift (4: 18) to Paul in prison. But who 'sends' the apostle who is the founding father of a local congregation?

In Paul's understanding, the commission to preach the word and, by so doing, to bring into existence a community of believers, comes from the risen Lord. God revealed his Son to Paul in order that Paul 'might preach him among the Gentiles' (Gal. 1: 16). Apostleship for the founder of a church comes not from 'flesh and blood', i.e. from any human empowerment, but from divine revelation (Gal. 1: 16; cf. Matt. 16: 17). For Paul this revelation has been mediated by the risen Lord: 'am I not an apostle? Have I not seen Jesus our Lord?' (1 Cor. 9: 1). 'Seeing' Christ and being 'sent' by him constitute Paul's understanding of apostleship.

Apostleship and association with the earthly Jesus

The conception of an apostle as a witness to the resurrection is found in Acts (2: 32; 3: 15; 13: 31; 4: 33). However, there is also a more exclusive understanding of apostleship, which is most clearly expressed in the account of the election of Matthias. Peter considers as candidates for the office left vacant by the apostasy of Judas only those 'who have accompanied us during all the time that Jesus went in and out among us, beginning from the baptism of John until the day when he was taken up from us' (Acts 1: 21-2).

Although Luke's identification of 'the apostles' with 'the Twelve' (Luke 6: 13) is a later theological development, it is quite likely that during Paul's lifetime there were those who refused to acknowledge as an apostle in the full sense someone who had not been associated with the earthly Jesus. This would explain both Paul's defensiveness concerning his right to be considered an apostle and his sarcastic references to the 'super-apostles' (2 Cor. 12: 11; author's translation) and to 'James and Cephas (Peter) and John, who were reputed to be pillars' (Gal. 2: 9) of the Jerusalem community (cf. v. 6). Peter and John, the son of Zebedee, were among the Twelve (Mark 3: 16, 17 par.), whereas James was 'the Lord's brother' (Gal. 1: 19).

The difference between Paul's understanding of apostleship and the more exclusive understanding with which he had to contend concerns the relationship to the 'foundational events' of the Christian movement considered necessary for someone to be a 'founding father' of a Christian community. Christianity shares with the Israelite religion the belief that God reveals himself in the history of a people or a community. Israel had its beginnings in the Exodus from Egypt and in the gift of the law on Sinai. The subsequent history of the people was interpreted in the light of these events.

Christianity's foundational events were of quite a different character. On the one hand, there was the life and death of Jesus, whose memory was preserved within the community which venerated him. The other foundational event was a religious experience which occurred after Jesus' death and conveyed to those who received it a new insight into Jesus' identity. According to the list in 1 Cor. 15: 5, 7, 8, these persons included a follower of the earthly Jesus (Peter), a relative of Jesus, who had not been a disciple (James), and someone who had known of Jesus only through the Christian community which he persecuted (Paul).

Israel's memory of the Exodus was transmitted through the cultic re-enactment of the event in the Passover meal (Exod. 12: 1-27). Since Deut. 31: 10-13 prescribes that the law be read out at the Feast of Booths, this must have been a feast for the renewal of the covenant. The covenant concept is closely connected with the city of Shechem, where the principal temple was named El-berith ('God of the Covenant'; Judg. 9: 46; cf. 9: 4). Israel's foundational events were also remembered in confessions of faith, such as the one which every Israelite was to make when he presented the first fruits of the harvest at the sanctuary (Deut. 26: 5-11).

From the Easter experience to 'the word of faith'

The kerygmatic formulations and christological titles which we find in the New Testament derive from the foundational event of the Easter experience. This is obviously true of the affirmations of Christ's death and resurrection, but it is also true for titles such as 'Son of God' (cf. Mark 14: 36) and 'Christ' (cf. Mark 15: 2 par.), which may be rooted in Jesus' ministry or in his trial before Pilate. For these titles acquired new meaning through the Easter experience: as a result of the conviction that God had vindicated Jesus by raising him to his right hand, 'Christ' and 'Son of God' became expressions of Jesus' saving role after his death.

The New Testament affirms a sacramental incorporation of the believer into the Easter experience through baptism (Rom. 6: 1-14; Col. 2: 12) and a proclamation of Christ's death in the Lord's supper (1 Cor. 11: 26). However, the Easter experience itself is accessible to us only in linguistic form, that is, in the formulations and titles just mentioned. Now every linguistic articulation of an experience is already an interpretation: the person who has the experience must incorporate it into his own historical capacity for understanding, from which he draws the concepts and words he chooses to use. This is true even in the case of Paul, the only New Testament author who claims to have seen Christ after his death. Even he is obliged to express himself in traditional language, specifically the language of a prophetic vocation (Jer. 1: 5; Isa. 49: 1).

The pre-Pauline credo is a community formulation. That is to say, it does not necessarily reproduce the exact words used by either Peter or James to express their Easter experience. This experience, therefore, comes to us in two forms: in the words of someone who actually had it (Gal. 1: 15-16) and in a form which is probably the result of transmission within a Christian community (1 Cor. 15: 5, 7). In either case, we are dealing with the expression in language of ecstatic experiences.

The use of such formulations on the part of an apostle in preaching the gospel (1 Cor. 15: 1), and thereby founding a church, represents a crucial shift. Though the words remain the same, their function is now quite different. The expression of an ecstatic faith experience is used in the apostle's preaching to express 'the faith' which is to be communicated to a prospective convert; the latter is summoned to accept the kerygmatic formulation in obedience (Rom. 1: 5), whether or not he has had any personal experience of his own.

To be sure, the special endowments given by the spirit upon acceptance of Paul's preaching include ecstatic gifts such as prophecy and glossolalia (1 Cor. 12: 10). However, in this case the experience results from accepting the faith, whereas for Paul himself faith had resulted from the experience of seeing the Lord. Consequently, there arises a fundamental distinction between persons whose conversion to Christ was based upon an immediate religious perception and persons whose conversion consisted in becoming 'obedient to the standard of teaching' (Rom. 6: 17) proposed by the missionary. 'The word of faith' (Rom. 10: 8) has become the means of bringing to faith those whose own conversion consists in acknowledging Christ by means of a confessional formula (Rom. 10: 9) and undergoing baptism.

Obviously, a conversion experience is not incompatible with baptism. Paul, in associating himself with the baptized (e.g. 1 Cor. 12: 13), may imply that he has undergone this rite. However, the only explicit reference to Paul's baptism occurs in Acts 9: 18, and, for the author of Acts, Paul's missionary mandate, delivered by the Lord after Paul's conversion, is given not to Paul directly but to a representative of the Christian community, Ananias (vv. 15-16).

These two modes of coming to faith are contrasted in the words attributed by the Fourth Evangelist to the risen Jesus, as he addresses 'doubting Thomas': 'Have you believed because you have seen me? Blessed are those who have not seen and yet believe' (John 20: 29). Believing through seeing is the privilege of the apostles; for those who follow after, 'faith comes from what is heard' (Rom. 10: 17), i.e. the missionary preaching. We note a certain tension between these two understandings of belief in the writings of Paul, who, while fiercely defending his right to the apostolic title, acknowledges the unusual circumstances and timing of his apostolic vocation (1 Cor. 15: 8-9).

Paul insists that he has received his gospel directly through a revelation of Jesus Christ, and not by any human mediation (Gal. 1: 11-12). Nevertheless, when reminding the Corinthians of the gospel which they have received from him, he uses a formulation which he himself had 'received' (1 Cor. 15: 3). In other words, Paul affirms, in different contexts, both the mediacy and the immediacy of the gospel which he preaches: he has received it both through the church and directly from God. These conflicting affirmations bring out Paul's own peculiar situation: he saw the Lord several years after the Christian movement had begun.

At the beginning of his letter to the Romans, Paul combines a traditional hymnic confession of faith (1: 3-4) with a formulation of the gospel expressed in terms of his own conversion experience of the righteousness of God in Jesus Christ (vv. 16-17). His purpose in so doing appears to be to recommend himself to a community which he does not know personally. Before he expounds to the Romans his own personal gospel, he shows himself prepared to accept a traditional formulation.

'Believing through hearing'—'believing through seeing'

This tension between 'believing through hearing' and 'believing through seeing' is found in the greatest classic of wisdom literature in the Hebrew Bible, the Book of Job. After the hero encounters God in the whirlwind, he exclaims, 'I have heard of thee by the hearing of the ear, but now my eye sees thee' (Job 42: 5). The conception of God received from tradition, which is contained in the dogmatic assertions of Job's companions, had only driven the hero to more and more audacious outbursts of protest against his divine persecutor. But Job's direct personal experience of the living God gave him a vindication utterly different from the one which he had sought, a vindication which, paradoxically, leads to his repentance: 'therefore I despise myself and repent in dust and ashes' (42: 6).

The basis for apostolic authority

The basis for Paul's claim to apostolic authority is that he has seen the Lord (1 Cor. 9: 1), but the author of the letter to the Colossians warns his readers against anyone 'taking his stand on visions' (2: 18).

The insistence that there is a 'cut-off point' for seeing the risen Lord is all the more striking because this point is not uniformly set. The author of Acts, for whom Paul is not an apostle, except in the sense of a missionary emissary of the Antiochene church (14: 4, 14; cf. 13: 1-3), refers to the 'forty days' during which Jesus 'presented himself alive to [the apostles] after his passion by many proofs, appearing to them' (1: 3). In Luke's earlier volume, the appearances of the risen Lord seem to terminate on Easter Sunday (Luke 24: 51). In either case, Paul's experience before Damascus, though narrated on three occasions (Acts 9: 3-9; 22: 6-11; 26: 12-18), is evidently not included among the Easter appearances.

Paul, on the contrary, deliberately associates himself with those to whom Christ appeared, but he indicates that Christ's appearance to him was the last in the series: 'last of all, as to one untimely born, he appeared also to me' (1 Cor. 15: 8). If a resurrection appearance was possible two or even five years after Jesus' crucifixion (Paul's conversion is variously dated), there is no obvious reason why such appearances could not occur later still. Indeed, the accounts of the risen Lord's appearances in the Gnostic gospels (see pp. 151-2) convey a claim to access to continuing revelation through visions.

The need for a cut-off point becomes clear, however, if having seen the Lord is the basis for apostolic authority, since this would be completely relativized by continuing visions of the risen Christ, such as the Gnostics claimed. If this authority was to be limited to the Twelve (Luke-Acts) or to 'all the apostles' (1 Cor. 15: 7), including Paul (v. 8), then resurrection appearances must be correspondingly limited, whether by Christ's ascension (Luke-Acts) or by the Damascus experience (Paul).

Paul's authority in the churches he founded

After founding a community, Paul naturally assumed a decision-making role within the community. During the apostle's absence, members of the community appear to have assumed leadership roles, since Paul refers to 'functions of governance' (author's translation) at Corinth (1 Cor. 12: 28) and to 'presidents' (author's translation) in Thessalonika (1 Thess. 5: 12). Moreover, the first converts in a particular locality, whom Paul calls 'the first fruits'

(1 Cor. 16: 15; Rom. 16: 5), offered their homes for assemblies of the community and laboured on its behalf. Paul expects other members of the community to show obedience to such persons, in recognition of the service which they render (1 Cor. 16: 16; 1 Thess. 5: 12-13).

Such ministries of governance, which Paul lists among the spiritual gifts, stood in close relationship to his own apostolic ministry. He retained responsibility for the communities which he had founded and exercised this responsibility through periodic visitations, by sending his co-workers, Titus and Timothy, to function as his personal delegates, and through forceful epistolary interventions.

Tradition in earliest Christianity

Paul made use of traditional kerygmatic formulations in his instructions to his communities, and he seems to have laid some weight on the actual wording ('I would remind you, brethren, *in what terms* I preached to you the gospel' (1 Cor. 15: 1). However, his consciousness of his own apostolic authority made it unnecessary for him to rely upon such formulations in the way that Pauline communities felt obliged to do after he had passed from the scene. In the Pastoral Epistles, the formula, 'The saying is sure', is used five times (1 Tim. 1: 15; 3: 1; 4: 9; 2 Tim. 2: 11; Titus 3: 8) to affirm the truth of a statement concerning salvation. Such dependence on fixed faith statements is characteristic of a later stage in the history of Paul's churches, when they no longer had the apostle to guide them.

Paul himself, after instructing the Corinthians on the subject of divorce, in accordance with Jesus' teaching (1 Cor. 7: 10: 'not I but the Lord'), proceeds to give his *own* instruction (v. 12: 'I say, not the Lord') on the subject of 'mixed marriages' and other related matters. He concludes the section by expressing his conviction, 'I think that I have the spirit of God' (v. 40).

The apostle seems not to have regarded himself as confirmed in grace. He mentions the possibility that 'after having preached to others, I myself should be disqualified' (1 Cor. 9: 27). In underlining the irreformable character of his initial preaching to the Galatians, he even considers the hypothetical possibility that 'we should preach to you a gospel contrary to that which we preached to you' (Gal. 1: 8). Nevertheless, Paul recognizes no authority, even 'an angel from heaven' (Ga. 1: 8), which would be superior to that of his own gospel. His use of tradition, whether the Old Testament or traditional Christian formulations, was therefore free and original.

Jewish tradition was variously used in early Christianity. Josephus reports that when the high priest Annas took advantage of the death of Festus, the provincial procurator, to accuse and execute James, the brother of Jesus, 'those of the inhabitants of the city who were considered most fair-minded and who were strict in observance of the law were offended at this' (*Ant.* xx. 201). From James's reputation, even among non-Christian Jews, for his strict observance, we may infer that the Torah remained in force for Christians who recognized his authority.

Matthew's special tradition indicates that the 'oral Torah' taught by the Pharisees had been binding at some stage in the community's history (23: 3: 'practice and observe whatever they tell you'), even though the evangelist has Jesus warn the community against 'the leaven of the Pharisees and Sadducees' (16: 6), i.e. their 'teaching' (v. 12). From these two instances, the Jerusalem community and the community for which Matthew wrote, it is clear that Christian churches which remained within Judaism had greater respect than Paul did for Jewish tradition. Unlike him, they also adopted from the synagogue the authority of elders in community governance (cf. Acts 11: 30; 15: 2, 4, 6, 22, 23; 16: 4; 21: 18). (The word 'presbyter' never occurs in an authentic letter of Paul, although, according to Acts, he and Barnabas 'appointed elders in every church' (Acts 14: 23).)

As to the Jesus tradition preserved in the gospels, we have no clear idea how it was used during the first decades of the Christian movement, although the proclamation of Jesus' death and resurrection would scarcely have been credible without some indication of who Jesus was and what he had said and done. Paul refers explicitly to a saying or teaching of Jesus on only three occasions (1 Cor. 11: 23–5; cf. Luke 22: 19–20; 1 Cor. 7: 10–11; cf. Luke 16: 18; 1 Cor. 9: 14; cf. Luke 10: 7; Mark 2: 25–6), though teachings similar to those found in the gospels are contained in his writings. It is possible that he made greater use of the Jesus tradition in his initial instruction of the communities which he founded.

It would be reasonable to assume that Peter, who had been a companion of Jesus, used the Jesus tradition more extensively. Acts mentions Peter's activity outside Jerusalem, in Lydda, Joppa, and Caesarea (9: 32 - 10: 48), and after his escape from prison, 'he departed and went to another place' (Acts 12: 17), presumably to carry on missionary activity. Peter's missionary endeavours among the circumcised are confirmed by Paul (Gal. 2: 8), but we have no examples of his preaching. The sermons which he delivers in Acts are so similar in style to those delivered by Paul that we must assume that they are Luke's own creations. Whatever archaic elements they may preserve, there is nothing in them that can be identified as specifically Petrine. 1 Peter is a work of the Pauline school, whose attribution to Peter bears witness to the common veneration of the two martyr apostles at the time of its composition, but it cannot be used as a source for Peter's teaching. 2 Peter is probably the latest work in the New Testament canon; it was written some seventy years after Peter's death.

Nor do we have anything on which to base a judgement concerning the use of tradition by John, the son of Zebedee. Although he is represented as accompanying Peter in Acts, he is a silent partner. We do not even have Luke's rendering of what he might have said.

Paul and the apostles before him

Apart from church emissaries, these are the only apostles whom Paul mentions by name. At least, it seems probable that Paul regarded these three men as apostles. He declares that God 'who worked through Peter for the mission (*apostolēn*) to the circumcised worked through me also for the Gentiles' (Gal. 2: 8). In his account of his first trip to Jerusalem, Paul declares, after mentioning his visit with Cephas, 'I saw none of the other apostles except James the Lord's brother' (Gal. 1: 19). This suggests that James, as well as Peter, was an apostle in Paul's eyes. To be sure, the Greek can be translated 'but only' as well as 'except', but James's association with 'all the apostles' (1 Cor. 15: 7) suggests the other rendering. Paul makes no reference to John's apostolic credentials, but since he is associated with James and Peter as one of the 'pillars' of the Jerusalem community (Gal. 2: 9), and since, like Peter, he was one of the Twelve (Mark 3: 17 par.), Paul probably considered him among 'those who were apostles before me' (Gal. 1: 17).

How authoritative did Paul regard his apostolic teaching for communities which he had not founded? He appeals to the common acceptance by Peter (1 Cor. 15: 5), James (v. 7), and himself (v. 8) of the early credo (v. 11); did he regard his own doctrinal positions, especially his teaching on justification, as binding on the other apostles and on the communities which owed them allegiance?

Paul does not seem to have urged his personal theological convictions in his dealings with the Jerusalem authorities. The word 'law' does not occur in his summary of the 'apostles' council' (Gal. 2: 6-10). When writing to the church in Rome, Paul is extremely reticent in referring to his apostolic authority. He uses the title 'apostle' in the opening verse (Rom. 1: 1) and once in the body of the letter: 'an apostle to the Gentiles' (11: 13). The delicate way in which he expresses his hope for *mutual* spiritual benefit and encouragement, when he visits Rome (1 : 11-12), suggests respect for a community which has come to faith independently of him. Writing to the Philippians, Paul expresses his grief over those who 'preach Christ from envy and rivalry' (1: 15), proclaiming him 'out of partisanship, not sincerely, but thinking to afflict me in my imprisonment' (v. 17). But then, in an extraordinary outburst of apostolic magnanimity, he asks, 'What then? Only that in every way, whether in pretence or in truth, Christ is proclaimed, and in that I rejoice' (v. 18).

Of course, it would be anachronistic to regard Paul as a 'Christian pluralist' who regarded his interpretation of the gospel as one possible view among many. His reticence in dealing with the Jerusalem and Roman churches was motivated, no doubt, by practical considerations: he was more concerned with obtaining the good will needed to facilitate his missionary endeavours, than he was to attempt to impose his particular brand of Christianity on communities for which he was not personally responsible. On the other hand, he was not afraid of conflict, when he felt the truth of the gospel was at risk, and he did not hesitate to charge a fellow apostle, Peter, with hypocrisy (Gal. 2: 13).

Whatever his motivation, Paul seems to have given *de facto* recognition to the principle of territoriality, as far as doctrinal diversity was concerned. We might compare the formula adopted at the time of the Reformation, 'In a prince's country, the prince's religion.' In the apostolic age, an apostle's teaching was authoritative in his own sphere of influence. Paul's attacks on other Christians are reserved for those who teach what he considers erroneous doctrine within the communities which he has founded. The one clear exception proves the rule: Paul's abrupt departure, after the dispute with Cephas, from the Antiochene community, for which he had served as a missionary, is to be contrasted with his persistent and ultimately successful efforts to regain the loyalty and obedience of the church at Corinth, which he himself had founded.

The four apostles who appear in Paul's letters are all likely to have died during the sixties. Peter's martyrdom is mentioned explicitly by the author of the epilogue to the Fourth Gospel (John 21: 19). The martyrdom of James, the brother of the Lord, is narrated by Josephus (*Ant.* xx. 200). Although Luke leaves Paul preaching the gospel 'openly and unhindered' in Roman house arrest (Acts 28: 31), Paul's prediction to the Ephesian elders that they will see his face no more (Acts 20: 25) and their grief-stricken reaction (vv. 37-8) appear to presuppose his martyrdom.

Corresponding to Jesus' prophecy of Peter's death (John 21: 18) is his prophecy of the martyrdom of the sons of Zebedee (Mark 10: 39 par.). Of the two brothers, only James's death is recounted in the New Testament (Acts 12: 2). However, the martyrdom of John, the son of Zebedee, is no longer ruled out by John 21: 22-3, since many modern scholars do not identify him as 'the beloved disciple'. On the contrary, the anonymity of this figure, who is represented as the source behind the tradition of the Fourth Gospel, is characteristic of the second generation of Christian leaders, not one of whom is known to us by name.

The Twelve

The group to which both Peter and John belong, the Twelve, poses special difficulties for the historian. For Mark, the earliest evangelist, they are little more than a list of names (3: 16-19). This has led some scholars to doubt whether they actually existed, as a group, during Jesus' ministry. The mission of the Twelve (Mark 6: 7-13, 30), for which their constitution (3: 14: 'he appointed twelve') is the necessary presupposition, has been taken to be an inventive anticipation of the functions of the Easter mission, 'to preach and have authority to cast out demons' (Mark 3: 14-15). This suggestion becomes more plausible when we note that Mark appears to have no information about the 'pre-Easter mission'. Mark 6: 12-13a simply state the execution of Jesus' purpose, and v. 13b ('they anointed with oil many that were sick and healed them') is a striking anticipation of later church practice (Jas. 5: 14-15).

On the other hand, the role of the Twelve in the post-Easter community is equally elusive. Paul refers to them only once, in citing the pre-Pauline credo (1 Cor. 15: 5). He makes no mention of them in connection with his first visit to Jerusalem (35/38). Of course, this could be explained by his reluctance to acknowledge an inner group of apostles to which he would not belong. But it is also possible that by this time the Twelve, or at least some of them, had anticipated Peter in leaving Jerusalem to carry out missionary work elsewhere. Although the later traditions that the Twelve scattered to various corners of the world are apocryphal, the attribution to Thomas of a number of writings which originated in East Syria could be explained by the recollection of this apostle's missionary activity in the area.

There remains, however, the difficult problem of the status and function of the Twelve prior to their departure from the holy city. The saying in Matt. 19: 28 par. suggests that their significance was eschatological: 'you will sit on (twelve) thrones, judging the twelve tribes of Israel'. Were the Twelve somehow an early casualty of the failure of the expected imminence of the kingdom?

Although Luke highlights the power of 'the apostles' (= the Twelve) in Jerusalem, he tells us little about what they actually did there, and we cannot fill out the picture by drawing on the duties assigned to community officials at Qumran. The function of the Twelve in Acts may be primarily theological: they represent the apostolic centre from which all missionary activity in the Gentile church proceeds.

There is a clear tendency in the New Testament (Matt. 10: 2; Luke 6: 13; Rev. 21: 14) to identify the Twelve and the apostles, even though they appear as separate groups in the pre-Pauline credo (1 Cor. 15: 5, 7). Thus the church-founding role of the apostle is joined to the function of the Twelve as Jesus' companions (Mark 3: 14). The identification of the apostles with the Twelve bears witness to a concern to root the activity of the church in the ministry and intention of Jesus, at a time when the founding fathers were passing from the scene.

The second generation

The beginning of the Jewish War in 66 marks the end of the 'apostolic age' and a new period in the Christian movement, which had already expanded far beyond its place of origin in Palestine. The concern for tradition which characterizes this second generation of the movement is expressed, first of all, in the production of 'gospels'. (The use of the word in the plural to designate the first four books of the New Testament has no basis in the New Testament itself.)

The gospels

The first of these works, the Gospel according to Mark, was written around the year 70. Whether it was completed shortly before or shortly after the destruction of the holy city remains a matter of dispute. Although the author is clearly motivated by the need to encourage his community during a period of severe persecution, his pioneer accomplishment must also have been prompted by a concern to preserve in written form the quite disparate materials which his gospel contains. He does this by situating the narratives and sayings within a chronological framework of his own devising, which begins with Jesus' baptism and ends with the discovery of the empty tomb.

Mark's gospel contains only two extended discourses of Jesus, the Parable Discourse (4: 1-34) and the Apocalyptic Discourse (ch. 13). The amount of sayings material was greatly increased in two later 'editions' of Mark, namely, Matthew and Luke. These works were written about twenty years later, and they included additions from a collection of discourse material ('Q' = 'Quelle', German for 'source'), which is no longer extant as such. These two gospels also prefaced the account of Jesus' ministry with infancy narratives.

We know that the Fourth Gospel was written before the end of the century. A fragment from a manuscript which contained it (P^{52}) has been discovered in Egypt, and the style of handwriting in this fragment can be dated to the middle of the second century. Since the Fourth Gospel was already in general circulation in Egypt at such an early date (130-150 CE), it can scarcely have been written later than 100 CE. This last of the gospels maintains the general form of a 'life of Jesus', but it is so different from the synoptics in its chronology and in the tradition which it contains that scholars today still disagree as to whether the author or the tradition on which he depends had any direct knowledge of the three earlier works.

All four gospels share in the anonymity which is characteristic of second-generation Christianity. Not one of these works contains the name of its author. The titles by which they are now designated were added to the original works when they were brought together in a single manuscript, and it became necessary to distinguish them from each other.

To be sure, the author of the epilogue to the Fourth Gospel attempts to make the beloved disciple the author of chapters 1-20: 'this is the disciple who is bearing witness to these things, and *who has written these things*' (John 21: 24). However, nothing in the gospel itself confirms this affirmation. The statement in the crucifixion scene, 'He who saw [the piercing of Jesus' side] has borne witness—his testimony is true' (19: 35) is very probably an addition by the final redactor, designed to prepare the reader for his statement in 21: 24. But even if it is a comment of the evangelist, it only concerns the source of his tradition and presupposes a distinction between this source and the author himself.

Of the four apostles known to us from Paul's writings, only Peter has a major role in the gospels. James, the brother of Jesus, is mentioned in passing in Mark 6: 3 par. and, presumably, is to be included in the other references to Jesus' 'brothers' (Mark 3: 31 par.; cf. Mark 3: 21; John 7: 3, 5, 10). The sons of Zebedee appear in a vocation story at the beginning of Mark's gospel (1: 19-20 par.), which parallels the calling of another pair of brothers, Simon and Andrew (vv. 16-18). The two pairs of brothers reappear towards the end of the gospel to ask Jesus the question which elicits the Apocalyptic Discourse (Mark 13: 3). John, the son of Zebedee, also belongs to the inner group of three (the four brothers mentioned above, minus Andrew), who witness the raising of Jairus' daughter (Mark 5: 37 par.), the transfiguration (Mark 9: 2 par.), and Jesus in Gethsemane (Mark 14: 33 par.). But despite the appearance of these three apostles in the synoptics, there is no evidence of the influence of any apostolic figure or figures in the transmission of the material which they contain.

This is also true of the Fourth Gospel, even if the beloved disciple is taken to be a follower of Jesus during his ministry, since this anonymous figure is nowhere awarded the title 'apostle'. The word occurs only once in the gospel, in a proverbial saying: 'nor is he who is sent (*apostolos*) greater than he who sent him' (John 13: 16). But we may go further and question whether the beloved disciple need have been one of Jesus' original disciples at all. The phrase 'the disciple whom Jesus loved' does not necessitate this, since it does not express a human friendship, for which chronological contemporaneity is required. The beloved disciple is the 'ideal' disciple, not in the sense of being a fictitious figure—this is excluded by his competitive relationship with Peter—but rather in the sense of being the disciple who enjoys the most perfect union with Jesus. One may compare the relationship expressed in the angelic hymn: 'men on whom [God's] favour rests' (Luke 2: 14, NEB). Such a relationship is not dependent on the limitations of time and space.

If the beloved disciple is, in fact, an anonymous Christian leader from the second generation, then we may suppose that just as the author of the epilogue has tried to make him the author of the gospel, so the author of the gospel has tried to make him the source behind his work, by introducing him into the scenes of the Last Supper (John 13: 23), the crucifixion (19: 26), and the race to the tomb (20: 2). (The 'other disciple', who was 'known to the high priest' (18: 15) may be another such instance.)

The attempt to strengthen the reliability of the tradition behind the Fourth Gospel by eyewitness testimony is not an isolated example, and it is surely significant that, apart from Paul's appeal to eyewitness testimony for the truth of Jesus' resurrection (1 Cor. 15: 6), all the relevant New Testament passages come from writings datable to the last decade of the first century. Luke's appeal to 'eyewitnesses' (Luke 1: 2) is inseparable from his task of presenting the origins and claims of Christianity in a way which would attract the attention of cultivated people. For, as the introduction to many a Hellenistic historiographical work will show, eyewitness testimony, or, at least, the appeal to such testimony, was of cardinal importance in this type of writing. In urging the intimate connection of himself and his associates with 'the things which have been accomplished among us' (Luke 1: 1), Luke is simply following the convention of historians whose style he has undertaken to imitate.

The likelihood that the appearance of the beloved disciple in the Fourth Gospel may not express any historical relationship to Jesus is strengthened by the fact that the beloved disciple does not appear in the gospel until ch. 13, as well as by the curious unwillingness of the evangelist to identify him. Older attempts to identify the beloved disciple with John, the son of Zebedee, not only involve illegitimate harmonization of the Fourth Gospel with the synoptics but also ignore these two crucial data. The impossibility of reconciling John 19: 25-7 with the list of witnesses to Jesus' crucifixion given in the synoptics (Mark 15: 40-1 par.) has long been taken as an indication that the Johannine version is an 'ideal scene'. Moreover, the Johannine race to the tomb (John 20: 3-10) has a parallel in Luke 24: 12, in which version, however, only Peter appears.

The effort of the final redactor to make the beloved disciple the author of the gospel reflects a special concern of the Johannine community. The redactor has frequently been identified with the author of 1 John, who had to deal with Johannine Christians who denied that Jesus had come in the flesh (1 John 4: 2-3). Against such an interpretation of the Fourth Gospel, an appeal to the eyewitness testimony of someone who had seen blood and water come forth from the side of the crucified (John 19: 34-5) would be conclusive.

The device of introducing the beloved disciple into several scenes in the Fourth Gospel has a parallel in the Gospel according to

Matthew, in a change which may account for why this gospel was attributed to this particular member of the Twelve. In Mark the story of the vocation of a publican is connected with an unknown person named Levi (Mark 2: 14). In the Matthean version of this story, Levi's place is taken by Matthew (Matt. 9: 9).

Such certification of the tradition contained in the Fourth Gospel does not make it any more reliable than the tradition contained in the other three. Nevertheless, by the same token, it does not make it any less reliable. We must simply say that not only are the *authors* of all four gospels unknown; we cannot even name any individuals who were demonstrably responsible for transmitting the *traditions* which these works contain. Nevertheless, it remains obvious that just as Jesus is the most probable stimulus for the Jesus tradition, so his disciples, whoever they may have been, must have played a role in the initial preservation of this tradition.

The formation of the Pauline corpus

The anonymous codification of the Jesus tradition in our gospels took place at the same time as the formation of the Pauline corpus. The letter to the Colossians refers to a practice which may go back to the apostle's own day: 'when this letter has been read among you, have it read also in the church of the Laodiceans; and see that you read also the letter from Laodicea' (4: 16). Not only were Paul's letters exchanged among the communities which received them; they were also edited by the communities to which they were sent. This redactional phase in the formation of the Pauline corpus is reflected in three works which represent more than a single letter: Philippians (two or three letters); 2 Corinthians (as many as five letters); Romans (ch. 16 is a separate letter of recommendation).

The appeal to apostolic authority

Not only were Paul's authentic letters collected, redacted, and exchanged; additional letters were written under Paul's name. This was another device by which second generation Christianity sought to preserve the link with its 'apostolic' origins: an appeal to apostolic authority to justify contemporary belief and practice. Again, the parallel with Matthew's gospel is instructive. In this gospel, the church, that is, the local community of Christian believers, is the ultimate authority for resolving disputes: if a person 'refuses to listen to [two or three witnesses], tell it to the church; and if he refuses to listen even to the church, let him be to you as a Gentile and a tax collector' (Matt. 18: 17). The power of binding and loosing (Matt. 18: 18), which may refer to either doctrinal or disciplinary decisions, is vested in the disciples (v. 1), that is, the community of believers as a whole.

However, in the parallel passage in ch. 16, this power is conferred by Jesus on Peter (v. 19), who, as a recipient of heavenly revelation (v. 17), takes the place of 'the Pharisees and Sadducees' (16: 12) as the authoritative teacher of the community. Of course, by the time Matthew's gospel was written, Peter had been dead for thirty years, and despite Roman Catholic interpretation of these verses, nothing in them suggests the presence in the Matthean community of someone who has succeeded to Peter's authority. Rather, the actions of the community are ratified by an appeal to an apostle who has seen the Lord. (The words 'flesh and blood has not revealed this to you' (Matt. 16: 17) recall Paul's account of his Damascus experience, in which he contrasts God's revelation to him of his Son with conferring with 'flesh and blood' (Gal. 1: 16).) Peter's apostolic authority, based on his having seen the Lord, is the assurance for the Matthean community's teaching and practice.

However little we know of Peter's career in the post-Easter community, he was clearly a figure of importance, which is in keeping both with his portrayal in the synoptic gospels as the spokesman for the Twelve and with the tradition that he was the first male disciple to have seen the risen Lord. His conduct at the dispute in Antioch indicates that he rejected both the legalistic rigorism of James and Paul's radical hostility to the law. He was therefore an authority figure who would be naturally attractive to the author of Matthew's gospel, who was seeking to lead a community with a tradition of Jewish particularism towards active involvement in a world-wide mission to Gentiles (Matt. 28: 19).

The author of Matthew's gospel and the authors of the Deutero-Pauline letters are doing the same thing: they invoke the authority of an apostle to justify the belief and practice of the community.

However, the strategy is different: Matthew's gospel introduces an appeal to apostolic authority into a codification of Jesus tradition which was originally anonymous; the Deutero-Pauline writers compose works which they attribute to Paul. In the latter case, anonymity is still involved, but it is not anonymous Jesus tradition. Rather, the authors preserve *their* anonymity through a pseudonymous appeal to the authority of Paul.

The Johannine community and the Jesus tradition

This appeal to apostolic authority is quite different from the way in which Johannine Christianity sought to maintain continuity with Jesus, and this difference is best explained by the historical situation of the beloved disciple, who was the authority figure for Johannine Christianity. If he was, in fact, a distinguished leader of the second generation, then he was even further removed from the foundational events of Christianity than was the apostle Paul. If Paul had not been a follower of the earthly Jesus, he at least had had an experience which he ranked among the Easter appearances to the apostles. The beloved disciple, however, could make no such claim to having seen the Lord. Only in the epilogue to the Gospel is such a claim made on his behalf (John 21: 7).

In the gospel itself, there is a scene in which, as in ch. 21, the beloved disciple appears together with Peter. Here the beloved disciple comes to faith not through an Easter apparition but through a visit to the empty tomb, where 'he saw the linen cloths lying' (John 20: 5). In his reaction (v. 8: 'he saw and believed'), the beloved disciple is contrasted implicitly with Peter, of whom no faith response is reported.

The beloved disciple is also implicitly compared with 'doubting Thomas'. If the beloved disciple is taken to be 'one of the Twelve' (John 20: 24), then the beatitude, 'Blessed are those who have not seen and yet believe' (v. 29), is difficult to understand, since it excludes the beloved disciple, the disciple *par excellence*. For he would then be in the same situation as Thomas, of whom Jesus asked reproachfully, 'Have you believed because you have seen me?' (John 20: 29). But if the beloved disciple is a second generation Christian, then he is included among those 'who have not seen [me] and yet believe' (v. 29). The Easter experience, upon which the apostolic title rests, is not a special privilege, as it was for Paul. From the perspective of this particular kind of second generation Christianity, the need for such an experience expresses the deficiency of the faith which is based on it. What the beloved disciple sees in the concluding chapter of the gospel proper is not the risen Lord but the grave cloths and their meaning, which remained hidden from the apostle Peter, who was the first to see the Lord.

Such intuitive insight into the sign value of incidents connected with Jesus' life and death is characteristic of the faith of the Johannine community, which needs neither the Easter experience nor apostolic testimony to this experience, in order to believe. The manner in which the community of the beloved disciple related its beliefs to Jesus was quite different from the ratification of community belief and practice in the Deutero-Pauline letters and the Gospel according to Matthew, which both appealed to apostolic authority.

In the community of the beloved disciple, the testimony of the spirit guides believers into all truth (John 16: 13), by revealing to them the true meaning of the scripture (20: 9) and the deeper meaning of the sayings and actions of Jesus preserved in the tradition, as well as of those mysterious signs narrated in connection with his death and burial. From this type of knowledge Peter, as the representative of 'apostolic' Christianity, remains excluded. For Johannine Christians, the spirit, not some apostolic figure from the past, brings to remembrance all that Jesus has said (John 14: 26). The community, following the example of the beloved disciple, perceives the true significance of Jesus' words and actions by remembering, under the spirit's inspired guidance, what Jesus has said (John 2: 22) and the scriptures' testimony concerning him (2: 17; 12: 16).

In this form of Christianity, discipleship is a matter of personal relationship to Jesus, rather than of membership in a community of apostolic foundation. Writers have commented on the individualism of Johannine Christianity. The Johannine community, unlike the ones founded by Paul, does not consist of members who are mutually interdependent. Each sheep hears the shepherd's voice for himself (John 10: 3, 16), and each branch is rooted directly in the vine (15: 4-7).

There is really only one command in the Johannine community, and that is to love like-minded Christians. This love, like the love of Jesus for the beloved disciple, is not an emotion; it is an expression of the union of those who love Jesus in the proper way—who believe in him as the pre-existent one who has come down from above. Although this love must express itself in action, even to the limit of Jesus' own sacrifice of himself (John 13: 15), it is not directed towards the community as such. Nowhere in the Johannine writings do we find anything equivalent to the Pauline notion of 'edification': the building up of the community through the labour, self-sacrifice, and example of its members. Matthew's gospel affirms, 'you will know them by their fruits' (7: 16), but for the Johannine community, the only thing that bears fruit is remaining in Jesus (John 15: 4).

Although this community is referred to twice as a 'church' (3 John 6, 9), it is clearly a church of quite a different character from those founded by Paul or addressed by the synoptic evangelists. Nor is 'the elder' (3 John 1) a member of a governing body such as presided over the Jerusalem church. Rather, he exercises his influence through letters and messengers over a wide circle of communities. In so doing, he comes into conflict with Diotrephes, who exercises monarchical powers within a particular community and refuses to acknowledge the elder's authority (3 John 9). The elder does not rely on arguments but intends a direct confrontation (v. 10).

In the Johannine community, the appeal is not to the authority of an apostolic figure from the past but to the spirit who is present to the true believer. Just as the Johannine Jesus declares before Pilate, 'Everyone who is of the truth hears my voice' (John 18: 37), so the elder is convinced that his readers will know that his testimony is true (3 John 12). Such a claim to direct access to the truth, through the spirit, was responsible in time for the sharp internal divisions which characterize Johannine Christianity.

The Johannine community's acceptance of apostolic authority

The First Letter of John is written against persons who claim to know God but do not acknowledge Christ come in the flesh or the sinfulness of their own lives. Both the author of the epistle and those whom he attacks appear to know and to profess the Johannine tradition, as contained in our present Fourth Gospel or in some earlier version of this work. However, they interpreted the Johannine gospel in mutually exclusive ways, and since they both appealed to the witness of the spirit, there was no way to determine which of these interpretations was 'correct'. In a community which had no awareness of the symbolic character of religious language, there was no possibility of reconciling the absolute commitment of faith with a recognition of the limited perspective of the individual.

Undoubtedly, the occasion for these divisions was the death of the beloved disciple, which caused particular consternation in the community since it was expected that he would 'remain' until the Lord's return (John 21: 22-3). Probably the beloved disciple's leadership had provided the same sort of balance for the individualism of his tradition which Paul's apostolic authority had given, during his lifetime, to the charismatic model of the communities which he had founded. Without this leadership, the conflicting interpretations of the Johannine tradition, both appealing to the immediate witness of the spirit of truth, were tearing the community apart.

It is in this context that we must read the First Letter of John, the epilogue to the Gospel, and, perhaps, certain other redactional additions to the Gospel as well. In 1 John we find the word *koinōnia* ('communion'), which was to become of such importance for the ecclesiology of the patristic and later periods. Only here in the New Testament is it used to express the relationship which exists among believers. How closely the 'horizontal' fellowship of the faithful among themselves is connected with the 'vertical' fellowship with God and Christ is shown in 1 John 1: 3. The author manifests the fellowship which he has with the Father and the Son, in order that his readers may have fellowship with him. In other words, the foundation of the fellowship between the author and his addressees is the fellowship of the author with God and Christ (cf. vv. 1-2).

This ecclesiastical fellowship has been broken by the 'antichrists' (1 John 2: 18)—those whose views the author is rejecting. 'They went out from us, but they were not of us; for if they had been of us, they would have continued with us; but they went out, that it might be plain that they all are not of us' (v. 19). 'Continuing with us' and 'going out from us' express, respectively, adherence to the truth (v. 21) and departure from the truth.

This appeal to church fellowship should be seen together with the author's insistence on public confession of faith. Since the author has come to realize that a 'believing' which admits no authority except that of the spirit is beyond any community control, he instructs his readers, 'By this you know the spirit of God: every spirit which confesses that Jesus Christ has come in the flesh is of God, and every spirit which does not confess Jesus is not of God' (1 John 4: 2). As with Paul, the confessional formula is made the test of whether or not one is speaking under the influence of the spirit of God (cf. 1 Cor. 12: 3).

It is not unlikely that this emphasis on the public aspect of Christian faith may have had an influence on the final redaction of the gospel. Where the sense of community is weak, the need for giving sacramental expression to the community is absent. Conversely, the strengthening of community ties, promoted in 1 John, may have led to sacramental additions to the gospel. If, for the evangelist, being born of the spirit was the necessary and sufficient condition for entrance into the kingdom of God, in the final redaction of the gospel there is a clear reference to baptism: 'unless one is born of *water and* the spirit, he cannot enter the kingdom of God' (John 3: 5). If, for the evangelist, Jesus is 'the (living) bread which came down from heaven' (John 6: 51a, 58), that is, heavenly wisdom, for the final redactor he is also the eucharistic bread which the believer must eat, in order to have eternal life (vv. 51b-7). The realism of this passage (v. 55 'my flesh is food indeed') seems to be undercut by the statement in v. 63, 'the flesh is of no avail', which could represent the viewpoint of the evangelist. Such hypothetical additions of an 'ecclesiastical redactor' would be in keeping with the shift within the Johannine tradition which 1 John represents.

The addition of the epilogue to the gospel, however, is not hypothetical. John 20: 30-1 clearly represents the conclusion of the original work. And it is precisely in the epilogue that we see the Johannine community accepting the principle of apostolic authority, which was needed to moderate the conflict of interpretations unleashed by the appeal to the spirit and the death of the beloved disciple. In ch. 21 Peter and the beloved disciple appear together, as they did in the race to the tomb (John 20: 3-10), but now the contrast between the two is no longer so disadvantageous for Peter. On the contrary, the embarrassment of the Johannine community over the demise of their leader, whose martyrdom is not mentioned and who appears to have died of natural causes (vv. 22-3), is underlined by the contrast with the death by which Peter had glorified God (vv. 18-19). But the ecclesiological significance of the scene lies in the clear acceptance of Peter's pastoral role, even though this role is expressed in terms of the commandment to 'love one another' so characteristic of the Johannine tradition (vv. 15-17). Here we see represented in narrative form the *rapprochement* between Christian communities which appealed to apostolic authority for their beliefs and practices and the type of Christianity represented by the Johannine tradition, which sought for truth in the immediate witness of the spirit but found itself unable to resolve the dissensions within the community which followed the death of the beloved disciple.

Luke-Acts

Nevertheless, the conflict between the witness of the spirit to the individual and the decisions of apostolic authority has continued throughout the history of the Christian church. In Luke-Acts we find an attempt to 'solve' the problem in a radical fashion which has not found acceptance in subsequent Christian history. Here the gift of the spirit, and the enthusiastic phenomena which accompany it, are restricted to the apostolic age. Charismatic endowments are given to the church by God only for the very special and unrepeatable period of its beginnings. In this particular solution, Jesus' promise of the spirit (Acts 1: 4-5) finds its fulfilment in the apostolic age; subsequent generations of Christians find their way to the kingdom by continuing in the faith which the spirit-filled apostles have taught (Acts 14: 22; cf. 15: 28).

Luke-Acts represents an understanding of Christianity so similar to what we find in the Pastoral Epistles that it has been argued that all five books must have the same author. Nevertheless, although apostolic authority is involved in both cases, in the Pastorals appeal is made to the authority of Paul, whereas in Luke-Acts, Paul, though a great missionary, is not an apostle, except in the sense of an emissary of the Antiochene church. Here apostolic authority is the authority of 'the apostles', meaning the Twelve.

Although, with the exception of Peter, none of the Twelve seems to have played any lasting historical role, their theological significance as the foundation for the church universal finds clear expression in Acts. This points ahead to the use of their authority in an early Christian manual on morals and church practice entitled 'The Teaching of the Lord through the Twelve Apostles' (the *Didache*). The 'foundational' role assigned to the Twelve in Luke-Acts also finds expression in the formation of the canon itself. Although it was the content of the twenty-seven books, as perceived through second- and third-century eyes, which recommended them for canonical status, it was necessary, in keeping with the tendency already noted for second-generation Christianity, to create apostolic credentials for them, where these did not already exist.

Fourteen New Testament books—just over half the total number of twenty-seven—belong to the Pauline corpus, that is, they are connected with Paul's apostolic authority by either real or pseudonymous authorship. Two more are associated with him through 'Luke', one of his 'fellow workers' (Philem. 24), i.e. the third gospel and Acts. But ten of the remaining books are attributed to five members of the Twelve: Matthew (Matt.), Peter (1-2 Pet.), John (John, 1-3 John, Rev.), James (Jas.), and Jude (Jude). In three instances this process was facilitated by the fact that the author, real or pseudonymous, had the same name as one of the Twelve (the pseudonymous authors of the Epistles of James and of Jude; the real author of Revelation: John, the seer). Finally, Mark's gospel is attributed to Peter's 'son' (1 Pet. 5: 13).

The second generation paved the way for this development, in so far as the authority of a living apostle, such as Peter or Paul, was replaced by the codification of an anonymous Jesus tradition, on the one hand, and by a body of pseudonymous literature, on the other. In both instances there is an appeal to the authority of apostolic figures from the past: to Paul, in the Deutero-Pauline letters; to Peter, in the Gospel according to Matthew; to the Twelve in Luke-Acts.

This method of legitimating evolving faith and practice is not to be judged by modern ethical standards. In an age which knew nothing of 'the development of doctrine', the only way for Christian faith to retain its authority as divine revelation was to demonstrate its identity with 'the faith which was once for all delivered to the saints' (Jude 3). Until the crucial point was reached at which church leaders claimed to possess apostolic authority *in their own persons*, as 'successors of the apostles' (cf. I. Clement 44. 1-2) (see p. 83), the appeal to apostolic figures from the past was the only way to establish this identity. After this point was reached, circulating one's own writings under the name of an apostle became an ecclesiastical offence.

The Pastoral Epistles

A milestone on the way to this development is represented by the Pastoral Epistles. Since the addressees (Timothy and Titus) are as pseudonymous as the author (Paul), we do not need to see behind them a monarchical bishop presiding over the communities which are actually addressed. Rather, the authority seems to lie in the hands of a group of 'elders' (1 Tim. 5: 17-20; Titus 1: 5-6). The sudden switch in Titus 1: 5, 7 from 'elders' to 'overseer' (RSV has 'bishop')—in the singular—has raised the question whether *episkopos* (cf. 1 Tim. 3: 1-7) may not simply designate a function exercised by a *presbyteros* (cf. Acts 20: 17, 28).

The duties assigned the presbyter-bishops include the preservation and transmission of the apostolic teaching (1 Tim. 6: 20), administrative responsibility for the congregation (1 Tim. 3: 4-5), and judicial oversight (1 Tim. 5: 19-20), especially where false teaching is involved (Titus 3: 9-10). The presbyter-bishops should seek to win over, by their teaching, those infected with heresy (2 Tim. 2: 25).

Although this form of church government is often seen as a stepping stone towards the mono-episcopate first attested in Ignatius of Antioch (*c.*35-107), the presbyter-bishops in the Pastorals do not exercise a sacramental role. They represent a fusion between the presbyteral form of church government, taken over from the synagogue by Jewish Christian communities, and the *episkopoi*, who are mentioned, together with the *diakonoi* ('deacons') in the opening verse of Paul's letter to the Philippians (1: 1). The *episkopoi* probably exercised a leadership role within the Philippian community during Paul's absence.

The office of presbyter-bishop is conferred by the laying on of hands (1 Tim. 4: 14; 2 Tim. 1: 6). The idea that a spiritual power is conferred through an external rite has been seen as an anticipation of the Catholic principle, that the legitimacy of the office ultimately guarantees the authenticity of the proclamation. However, in the Pastorals the office still remains subordinate to the 'good confession' of faith (1 Tim. 6: 12).

At this point in the development, there was as yet no external criterion by which to test the authenticity of the proclamation. Today all main-line Christian traditions have an extrinsic authority which they regard as necessary and/or sufficient for resolving disputes of belief and practice between Christians: the canon of scripture, the creeds, the ecumenical councils, the ecclesiastical magisterium. But even as late as the Pastorals (*c.*100), there was no norm of faith or practice which was considered universally binding on all those who invoked Christ's name.

Although we may see in the mentality exhibited in the Pastorals the harbinger of later 'orthodoxy', we must remember that the positions taken in these letters could only claim authority within the communities to which they were addressed. Consequently, what is branded as falsehood by the author of the Pastorals may have been perfectly acceptable teaching in some other church. Even writings which show such close affinities as Luke-Acts and the Pastorals differ as to whether or not Paul himself is to be considered an apostle.

Relations between Christian communities

Our knowledge of Christian communities of the second generation comes to us through works written to and for these communities. This means that we have little evidence for the relationships which existed *between* communities during this period. In this regard, we are better informed for the earlier period through the letters of Paul. Although, with the exception of Romans, these letters were written to his own churches, we are able to infer a good deal from them about Paul's relations with the churches in Jerusalem, Antioch, and Rome.

But from the fact that the New Testament has not preserved any polemical writings written by one community leader against another (except for 'the elder's' criticism of Diotrephes (3 John 9-10)) we should not conclude that the relations between Christian churches in this period were any less free from tensions and differences than in the apostolic age. There are two probable examples of Christian groups at odds with each other on fundamental issues. A criticism of the inadequate christology of Jewish Christianity may be expressed in the reference in the Fourth Gospel to the believers in Jerusalem to whom Jesus did not entrust himself (John 2: 23-4). The disagreements which existed between Paul and James during their lifetime are reflected in the Letter of James, in which Paul's teaching on justification by faith, or, at least, some caricature of it, is rejected in favour of an understanding of the relationship between faith and works which is closer both to rabbinic tradition and to the stance of early Catholicism (2: 14-26).

The Christian life

A similar tendency to moralism is discernible in the Pastorals, in which the behaviour of a Christian differs in no way—apart from the religious motivation on which it is based—from the 'bourgeois morality' expected of any respectable Roman citizen. The organizational changes reflected in these letters have replaced Paul's charismmatic community with one clearly divided into groups: presbyter-bishops and deacons, on the one hand; 'laity', on the other. Such a development was inevitable in the post-apostolic age. During Paul's lifetime, he was obliged to chide the Corinthians for their spiritual excesses and to remind them that 'God is not a God of confusion but of peace' (1 Cor. 14: 33). It should not surprise us, therefore, that in a later period, when the apostle's direction was no longer available to his communities, more organized structures became necessary on the local level. The charismatic community was unable, after Paul's death, to provide an enduring structure of internal and inter-church relationships. Similarly, the sharp transition from the complex subtleties of Pauline thought to the commonplace dogmatism and moralism of the Pastorals reflects the fact that traditionalist exponents of 'community theology' have assumed the mantle of a daring theological innovator.

Gnosis

The theological and organizational shifts reflected in the Pastorals are sometimes judged to have been the necessary response to the threat of 'what is falsely called knowledge (*gnosis*)' (1 Tim. 6: 20). Gnosis, the forerunner of later Gnostic systems, is an umbrella term used to cover a variety of cosmological and soteriological speculations. It is misleading to think of it as though it were a religion completely distinct from Christianity. It is quite likely that its origins are to be found in Jewish speculation on the first chapters of Genesis, and such speculation flowed naturally into Christianity from the parent faith. Many books of the New Testament have been profoundly influenced by Gnosis, and Paul himself makes use of its terminology when he proposes to the Corinthians a 'wisdom among the mature' (1 Cor. 2: 6).

The Pastorals are to be distinguished from Paul, and from Colossians and Ephesians as well, not so much by their opposition to Gnosis as by the manner of their opposition. The author makes no attempt to refute false teaching (contrast 1 Cor. 15: 12-19, 29-34) or to remind the community of the original *kerygma* which they have accepted in faith (contrast 1 Cor. 15: 1). He simply declares, 'If anyone does not agree with the sound words of our Lord Jesus Christ and the teaching which accords with godliness, he is puffed up with conceit, he knows nothing' (1 Tim. 6: 3-4). Such a person is to be admonished once or twice; if he remains obdurate, he is to be simply avoided (Titus 3: 10).

The criticism of Gnosis in the Pastorals is the inevitable reaction on the part of an institutionalized form of Christianity to an understanding of Christian faith which was basically indifferent to confessional formulations and to church structures. Unlike the Johannine Christians, the Gnostics appear to have been tolerant of those with differing views and were content to remain within church structures, until they were expelled by the Great Church, i.e. the early form of Catholic Christianity championed by writers such as Irenaeus (*c.*130-200). However, like the individualist Johannine Christians, prior to the crisis reflected in 1 John, the Gnostics did not *need* church structures in order to exist, and it is not surprising that such elitism posed an insupportable challenge to local church authorities.

The Gnostics, like the Fourth Evangelist, rejected a dependence on apostolic testimony. They maintained that, for pneumatics, knowledge of the truth, which was understood to be knowledge of one's own true self, was available without need for ecclesiastical mediation. In contrast, the second-generation Christianity represented in the New Testament canon was suspicious of personal insight and experience, and was concerned to contain them within the limits of a gradually emerging 'rule of faith'. Such a concern recalls Paul's admonition to prophets that they should exercise their charism 'in proportion to our faith' (Rom. 12: 6).

If Johannine Christianity only survived by merging with the Great Church, Gnostic Christianity did not survive at all, except in the pitiful Mandean community, which still exists south of Baghdad. To the Gnostics, the institutions of early Catholicism may have been 'dry canals' (*Apocalypse of Peter* 79. 30, in *The Nag Hammadi Library*, ed. J. M. Robinson, p. 343), but, in retrospect, the emergence of orthodoxy and the concomitant process of institutionalization appear as necessary prerequisites for the preservation of historical Christianity. In a sense, history has answered the critics of early Catholicism.

Conclusion

It would be difficult to reconcile the continuing validity of the New Testament canon, in all its diversity, with the view that the early Catholicism expressed in Luke-Acts and the Pastorals represents a definitive watershed in Christian history, from which no retreat is possible. On the other hand, the religious ideas of 'the one true church' and 'the one saving gospel' continue to exercise a numinous attraction which defies all historical demonstrations of the pluralism which actually existed within early Christianity.

Moreover, practically all Christian churches today have some form of church order and of tradition—at least a tradition of scriptural interpretation. Thus, despite the diversity which characterizes contemporary Christianity, it is heir to these two emphases of early Catholicism. The religious individualism of both the Johannine community and the Gnostics may have descendants in medieval alchemy and modern depth psychology, but once the memory of Jesus and the Easter experience became crystallized in set formulas, to be passed on to prospective converts, the way was open to a view of the church as 'the pillar and bulwark of the truth' (1 Tim. 3: 15). It was to be in this ecclesiastical form that Christianity would influence subsequent religious history.

BIBLIOGRAPHY

Books of General Usefulness

C. K. Barrett, *The New Testament Background: Selected Documents*, London 1961.

J. D. G. Dunn, *Unity and Diversity in the New Testament: An Inquiry into the Character of Earliest Christianity*, London 1977.

V. A. Harvey, *The Historian and the Believer: The Morality of Historical Knowledge and Christian Belief*, New York 1966. An attempt to clarify the theological problem of faith and history.

H. Koester, *Introduction to the New Testament* (2 vols.), Philadelphia 1982. The Jewish and Greco-Roman background of the New Testament; a treatment of methodological questions and a discussion, in their historical context, of more than sixty early Christian writings.

W. G. Kümmel, *Introduction to the New Testament*, London 1975. Probably the best available account of such matters as authorship and date.

D. Nineham, *The Use and Abuse of the Bible: A Study of the Bible in an Age of Rapid Cultural Change*, London and New York 1976. A provocative defence of the continuing significance of the Bible in an age of cultural and historical relativism.

J. M. Robinson (ed.), *The Nag Hammadi Library in English*, New York, Hagerstown, San Francisco, London 1974. The writings, discovered in 1945, which give us our first direct knowledge of Gnostic interpretation of Christianity.

R. N. Soulen, *Handbook of Biblical Criticism*, Atlanta 1976. An introduction to the technical language and methodology of modern biblical scholarship.

R. A. Spivey and D. Moody Smith, Jr., *Anatomy of the New Testament: A Guide to its Structure and Meaning*, New York and Toronto [2]1974. Readable, recent, well-illustrated, reliable, and concise; has good bibliographies.

B. H. Throckmorton, Jr. (ed.), *Gospel Parallels: A Synopsis of the First Three Gospels*, Toronto, Camden, N. J., and London [3]1967.

G. Vermes, *The Dead Sea Scrolls in English*, Penguin Books [3]1968. Though without any direct connection with early Christianity, this Essene library provides numerous contemporary parallels to New Testament thought.

W. Wink, *The Bible in Human Transformation: Towards a New Paradigm for Biblical Study*, Philadelphia 1973. A provocative criticism of the sort of scholarship which has made the New Testament irrelevant to those most interested in it.

G. E. Wright, *Biblical Archaeology*, Philadelphia and London [2]1962.

G. E. Wright and F. V. Filson, *The Westminster Historical Atlas to the Bible*, Philadelphia 1945.

Additional Suggestions for Reading, Chapter by Chapter

Chap. 2: H. W. Bartsch (ed.), *Kerygma and Myth: A Theological Debate*, New York and Evanston 1961.

M. Bloch, *The Historian's Craft*, New York 1971.

R. Bultmann, *Jesus Christ and Mythology*, New York 1958.

E. H. Carr, *What is History?*, Harmondsworth 1978.

R. T. Fortna, *The Gospel of Signs*, Cambridge 1970.

B. Gerhardsson, *The Origins of the Gospel Traditions*, London and Philadelphia 1979.

M. Hengel, *Acts and the History of Earliest Christianity*, London 1979.

E. Käsemann, 'Sentences of Holy Law in the New Testament', in *New Testament Questions of Today*, Philadelphia 1969, 66–81.

E. V. McKnight, *What is Form Criticism?*, Philadelphia 1969.

D. Nineham, 'Eyewitness Testimony and the Gospel Tradition', *Journal of New Testament Studies*, vol.9, 1958, 13–25, 243–52; vol. 11, 1960, 253–64.

N. Perrin, *What is Redaction Criticism?*, Philadelphia 1959.

C. H. Talbert, *What is a Gospel?*, Philadelphia 1977.

V. Taylor, *The Formation of the Gospel Tradition*, London, Melbourne, Toronto, and New York [2]1935.

M. Wilcox, 'On Investigating the Use of the Old Testament in the New Testament', in *Text and Interpretation: Studies in the New Testament Presented to Matthew Black* (ed. E. Best and R. M. Wilson), Cambridge 1979, 231–43.

Chap. 3:   M. Black, 'Jesus and the Son of Man', *Journal for the Study of the New Testament*, 1, 1978, 4–18.

G. Bornkamm, *Jesus of Nazareth*, New York and London 1960.

S. G. F. Brandon, *Jesus and the Zealots*, Manchester 1967.

R. Bultmann, *Jesus and the Word*, New York 1958.

D. Catchpole, *The Trial of Jesus*, Leiden 1971.

N. A. Dahl, 'The Crucified Messiah' in *The Crucified Messiah and Other Essays*, Minneapolis 1974, 10–36.

M. D. Hooker, 'Christology and Methodology', *New Testament Studies*, 17, 1970–1, 480–7.

J. Jeremias, *The Eucharistic Words of Jesus*, London and Philadelphia 1966.

J. Jeremias, *The Parables of Jesus*, London 1975.

S. McFague [TeSelle], *Speaking in Parables: A Study in Metaphor and Theology*, Philadelphia 1975.

B. F. Meyer, *The Aims of Jesus*, London 1979.

N. Perrin, *Rediscovering the Teaching of Jesus*, New York and Evanston 1967.

J. A. T. Robinson, 'Elijah, John and Jesus' in *Twelve New Testament Studies*, Studies in Biblical Theology 34, London 1962, 28–52.

J. M. Robinson, *A New Quest of the Historical Jesus*, Studies in Biblical Theology 25, London 1970.

A. Schweitzer, *The Quest of the Historical Jesus*, New York 1968.

G. A. Wells, *Did Jesus Exist?*, London 1975.

W. Zimmerli and J. Jeremias, *The Servant of God*, Studies in Biblical Theology 20, London 1965.

Chap. 4:   J. D. G. Dunn, *Jesus and the Spirit*, Philadelphia 1975.

R. H. Fuller, *The Formation of the Resurrection Narratives*, New York and London 1971.

R. H. Fuller, *The Foundations of New Testament Christology*, New York 1965.

F. Hahn, *Mission in the New Testament*, London 1965.

J. Jeremias, *Jesus' Promise to the Nations*, Studies in Biblical Theology 24, London 1958.

W. Kramer, *Christ, Lord, Son of God*, Studies in Biblical Theology 50, London 1966.

W. Marxsen, *The Resurrection of Jesus of Nazareth*, London 1970.

C. F. D. Moule (ed.), *The Significance of the Message of the Resurrection for Faith in Jesus Christ*, Studies in Biblical Theology 8, London 1968.

G. N. Stanton, *Jesus of Nazareth in New Testament Preaching*, Cambridge 1974.

Chap. 5: G. Bornkamm, *Paul*, New York and London 1971.

W. D. Davies, *Paul and Rabbinic Judaism*, London 1970.

J. G. Gager, 'Some Notes on Paul's Conversion', *New Testament Studies*, 27, 1980-1, 697-704.

J. Munck, *Paul and the Salvation of Mankind*, London 1959.

E. P. Sanders, *Paul and Palestinian Judaism*, London 1977.

H. J. Schoeps, *Paul*, London 1961.

Chap. 6: C. K. Barrett, *The Signs of an Apostle*, Philadelphia 1972.

R. E. Brown, *The Community of the Beloved Disciple*, New York, Ramsey, and Toronto 1979.

R. E. Brown, K. P. Donfried, and J. Reumann (ed.), *Peter in the New Testament*.

R. E. Brown, *Priest and Bishop: Biblical Reflections*, Paramus, New York, and Toronto 1970.

F. Hahn, *The Worship of the Early Church*, Philadelphia 1973.

G. D. Kilpatrick, *The Origins of the Gospel according to St. Matthew*, Oxford 1946.

E. Pagels, *The Gnostic Gospels*, New York 1979.

E. Schweizer, *Church Order in the New Testament*, Studies in Biblical Theology 32, London 1961.

G. Theissen, *The First Followers of Jesus: A Sociological Analysis of Earliest Christianity*, London 1978.

S. G. Wilson, *Luke and the Pastoral Epistles*, London 1979.

INDEX OF PASSAGES CITED

GENERAL INDEX

Col. vs Paul on apostleship & vision 727
Wing John 21, 145